P9-CFS-179

Tools & Skills:
Workshop, Plumbing & Wiring

Complete Handyman's Library™
Handyman Club of America
Minneapolis, Minnesota

Published in 1995 by
Handyman Club of America
12301 Whitewater Drive
Minnetonka, Minnesota 55343

Published by arrangement with Cowles Creative Publishing, Inc.
ISBN 0-86573-743-6

Printed on American paper by
R. R. Donnelley & Sons Co.
00 99 98 97 / 5 4 3 2

CREDITS:
Created by: The Editors of Cowles Creative Publishing
and the staff of the Handyman Club of America
in cooperation with Black & Decker. **BLACK&DECKER**
is a trademark of Black & Decker (US), Incorporated
and is used under license.

Handyman Club of America:
    Book Marketing Director: Cal Franklin
    Book Marketing Coordinator: Jay McNaughton

Contents

Introduction 4
Workshop Tools 5
    Common Tips 6
    Basic Tools Set 8
    Hammers 10
    Fasteners 12
    Handsaws 16
    Planes & Chisels 18
    Sanders 22
    Drills 24
    Circular Saws 28
    Table Saws 32
    Power Miter Saws 38
    Routers 42
    Specialty Tools 46
Workshop Techniques 48
    Measuring & Marking 50
    Using Clamps 58
    Using Adhesives 72
    Sanding 78
Plumbing: Tools, Materials & Skills 81
    Tools for Plumbing 82
    Plumbing Materials 86
    Plumbing Fittings 88
    Working with Copper 90
    Cutting & Soldering Copper 92
    Using Compression Fittings 98
    Using Flare Fittings 100
    Working with Plastics 102
    Cutting & Fitting Plastic Pipe 104
    Working with Galvanized Iron 110
    Working with Cast Iron 114
Wiring: Tools, Materials & Skills 118
    Learn About Codes 119
    Tools, Materials & Skills 120
    Electrical Boxes 122
    Installing Electrical Boxes 124
    Wires & Cables 128
    Installing NM Cable 132
    Conduit 138
    Circuit Breaker Panels 142
    Connecting Circuit Breakers 144
    Circuit Maps for 24 Common Wiring Layouts 146
Index 158

Introduction

Any project becomes easy if you know which tools to use and the techniques for using them properly. In fact, having good tools and knowing how to use them well can be as much fun as building the project. *Tools & Skills: Workshop, Plumbing & Wiring* is a treasure of information about the tools you use in your home projects. It shows you the specific tools and necessary techniques for doing the best possible work with wood, plumbing and electricity.

The first section, Workshop Tools, presents all the tools used to cut, shape and connect wood, whether you are building woodworking projects in your workshop or doing rough or finish carpentry around the house. You see which essential tools should belong in your basic tool set. The major hand and power tools are demonstrated, from hammers and screwdrivers to routers, along with many tips and accessories that expand these tools' capabilities. Plus all of the appropriate blades, bits and fasteners are shown, so that you know exactly which to use. Also included are a few specialty tools, available at rental centers, that can be very useful in your projects.

Workshop Techniques is packed full of techniques, tips and jigs that will help you build your woodworking projects most effectively. You see quick and accurate techniques for measuring and marking. You also learn how to choose and use the right adhesives, along with the best clamping methods to make your glue-ups turn out perfectly. Plus you find sanding techniques and tips that will help you sand any project easily.

The next section, Plumbing: Tools, Materials & Skills, contains all the information you need to undertake any plumbing project, whether replacing a small section of old, corroded galvanized water supply line or installing new plastic drain pipes and copper water supply lines for a bathroom in an addition. All of the materials and tools you need to do these projects are shown, including the techniques for working with the types of pipe and fittings available.

Finally, Wiring: Tools, Materials & Skills provides everything you need to know to accomplish electrical projects. You learn how to plan and install new circuits for any new addition or remodeling project that will meet professional standards. The necessary tools and materials are shown, along with the proper techniques, so you can do safe and successful work.

This volume is a valuable guide for improving your tool skill level. Plus, it offers tips for making successful woodworking projects easier, and techniques for making major plumbing and electrical projects that will save you money. But most of all, this book will help you gain the satisfaction of building a project with the right tools and materials, and doing it well.

NOTICE TO READERS

This book provides useful instructions, but we cannot anticipate all of your working conditions or the characteristics of your materials and tools. For safety, you should use caution, care, and good judgment when following the procedures described in this book. Consider your own skill level and the instructions and safety precautions associated with the various tools and materials shown. Neither the publisher nor Black & Decker® can assume responsibility for any damage to property or injury to persons as a result of misuse of the information provided.

The instructions in this book conform to "The Uniform Plumbing Code," "The National Electrical Code Reference Book," and "The Uniform Building Code" current at the time of its original publication. Consult your local Building Department for information on building permits, codes, and other laws as they apply to your project.

Workshop Tools

The following pages offer numerous tips to help you get the most out of your hand and power tools.

Some hand tools can be modified to make convenient specialty tools. You can also build your own tool accessories, including a variety of cutting guides, to help make routine workshop tasks quicker and easier.

Tools must be kept clean and dry, and cutting blades should be sharpened regularly. Properly maintained, good-quality tools can last a lifetime.

Take the time to learn how to use your tools correctly. Practice your tool techniques on scrap materials, and consult a tool-use book or ask an experienced friend for advice if you are unsure of your skills.

Conquer Rust

Remove rust from metal surfaces with steel wool, using light machine oil as a lubricant. As you remove rust, wipe the spot frequently with a clean cloth to remove rust particles and steel wool fragments. Coat surfaces with light oil to prevent further rusting.

Rust Buster

Store hand tools in a drawer lined with a piece of scrap carpet moistened with light machine oil. The carpet prevents tools from getting scratched or nicked, and the oil prevents rusting. Discard the carpet if it becomes caked with sawdust and dirt.

Less Wetter Is Better

Use a dehumidifier to control dampness in a basement or other shop location. High humidity levels cause rust to form on tool surfaces and inside power tool motors.

Tale of the Tape

Coat the blade of a steel tape measure with paste wax. The wax keeps the tape retractor working smoothly, and prevents dirt and grease from sticking to the blade.

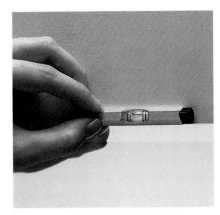

Small line level, designed for leveling masonry walls, is also handy for leveling pictures or mirrors on walls.

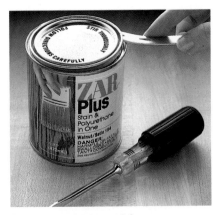

Do not use screwdrivers as chisels or prybars. A bent screwdriver shaft or a damaged tip can cause the screwdriver to slip and damage the workpiece.

Keep chisels and other cutting tools sharp. Forcing dull tools can be dangerous.

Make a dent with a center punch to start a hole in metal. This will encourage the bit to stay on target.

Use variable speed drill when drilling metal and keep rpms low to drill smoothly and to prevent dulling the bit.

Fit shop files with handles to provide a safe and comfortable grip when working on metal. A variety of file shapes will let you work on any object.

Use a hot glue gun to secure corner braces or reinforcements, or to fasten small objects that might split if nailed.

Do not use a claw hammer as an all-purpose tool. It is designed only for driving and pulling nails.

Clean the hammer face with sandpaper to remove residue caused by coated nails. This reduces the number of bent nails.

Framing square

C-clamp

Sanding block

Plumb bob/ chalk line

Nail sets

16-oz. claw hammer

Phillips screwdriver

Standard screwdriver

Mallet

2' carpenter's level

Putty knife

Chisel

Utility knife

Electronic stud finder

Cordless screwdriver

3/8" power drill

Drill bits

Combination square

T-bevel

Cat's paw

12' tape measure

Wonderbar®

Crosscut saw

Wallboard saw

Starter tool set should include a generous selection of hand tools, plus a ⅜-inch power drill and a cordless screwdriver. Inspect the finish on hand tools. Quality hand tools made of high-carbon steel are machined with clean-cut metal surfaces. Tool handles should be tight and comfortably molded.

Router

Circular saw

Palm sander

Jig saw

Plane

Caulk gun

Glue gun

Coping saw

A quality tool collection does not require a large initial investment. A home owner can build a tool collection by buying tools as they are needed for each carpentry project. Invest in top-grade tools made by reputable manufacturers. A quality tool always carries a full parts and labor warranty.

Read power tool specifications to compare features like horsepower, motor speed and cutting capacity. Better-quality tools also have roller or ball bearings instead of sleeve bearings, reinforced power cords, and heavy-duty trigger switches.

Intermediate tool collection includes additional power tools and special-purpose hand tools. Replace blades or resharpen cutting tools whenever they become dull.

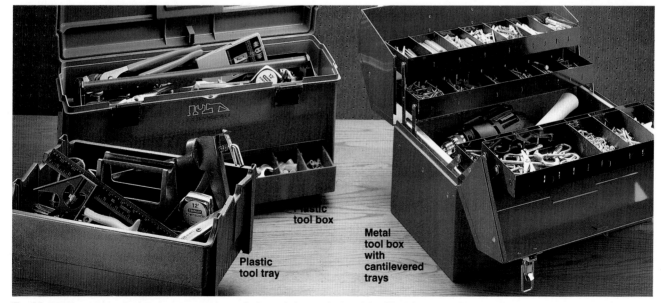

Plastic tool box

Metal tool box with cantilevered trays

Plastic tool tray

Tool boxes made of plastic or metal are lightweight and durable. Tool boxes with cantilevered trays and divided compartments keep tools and materials organized.

Two Claws in One

Nail notch

Small finish nails and brads can be difficult to pull with an ordinary hammer. Turn your claw hammer into a mini nail-puller by filing a ⅛" notch into one claw, using a triangular needle file (inset).

Grain of Truth

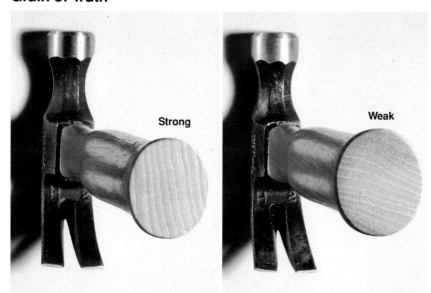

Strong

Weak

The strongest wooden tool handles have wood grain that runs parallel to the tool head (left). Handles with the grain running perpendicular to the tool head (right) are more likely to break. Check the end grain before buying a new tool or tool handle. Tool handles that are cracked or loose should be replaced.

Thumbs Up

To avoid hitting your thumb when hammering a small nail, push the nail through a piece of stiff paper, or hold it with a needlenose pliers or tweezers.

Easy Driver

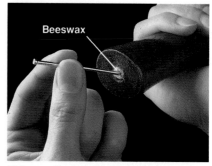

Beeswax

Drive nails into hard woods more easily by lubricating the nail points with beeswax. Keep a supply of wax handy by drilling a ¼" hole, ½" deep, in the end of your hammer handle and filling the hole with wax.

More Power to You

Remove stubborn nails by placing a block of wood under the hammer head for added leverage. Prevent damage to the workpiece by using a block big enough to distribute the pressure from the hammer head.

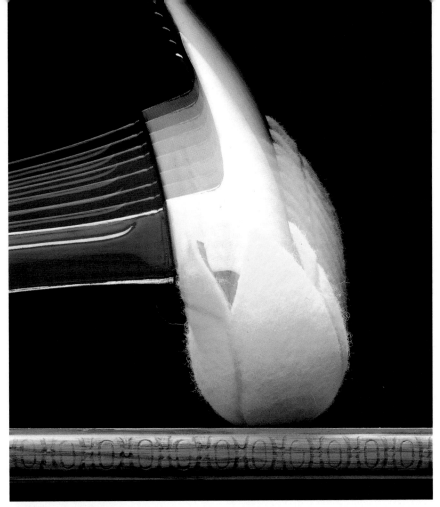

One-handed Nail Starter

Some situations require starting nails with one hand. Do this by wedging the nail in the claws so the nail head rests against the hammer head. Swing the hammer with the claws facing forward to start the nail, then loosen the claws from the nail and finish driving the nail with the striking face.

Soften the Blow

Using a standard metal hammer to tap wood joints into place can damage the workpiece. To avoid marring workpieces, convert your hammer to a soft-headed mallet. Cut a slit in a tennis ball, and slip it over the striking face of the hammer.

Surface Saver

Protect surfaces from hammer misses by slipping a piece of scrap pegboard over the nail and against the workpiece. When the nail is flush to the surface of the pegboard, remove the pegboard and finish the job with a nail set. Keep the striking face of the hammer clean by rubbing it with fine sandpaper. This will keep the face from slipping off the nail head.

Pulling Headless Nails

Pull headless nails by wedging the shank of the nail tightly in the claws and levering the hammer handle sideways. Inside edges of the claws must be sharp.

Sharpen Your Claws

Sharpen here

Inspect the hammer claws to make sure the tips and inside edges are sharp enough to grip nails. Sharpen dull claws with a flat metal file.

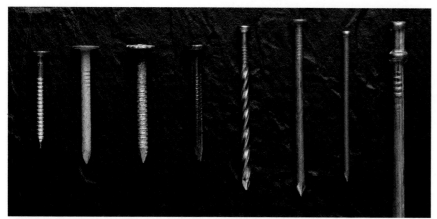

Nail assortment includes (left to right): wallboard nail, galvanized roofing nail, sealing roofing nail, concrete nail, hardwood flooring nail, common framing nail, finishing nail and double-headed form nail.

Predrill hardwood to avoid splitting it. Use a finishing nail as a drill bit for quick and accurate hole sizing.

Stagger nails so they do not all enter the same spot in the wood grain and split the wood.

Angling nails as shown will provide better holding power than driving them straight in.

Use the right hammer for superior job results. The tack hammer at rear is magnetized to hold tacks, and is lightweight to avoid damaging wood.

Toenailing is one method of joining two pieces of wood when end nailing is not possible.

Avoid damage to wood by using a nail set to drive the finish nail below the surface.

Use a brad pusher to position small nails in picture frames or other workpieces that might be damaged by a hammer.

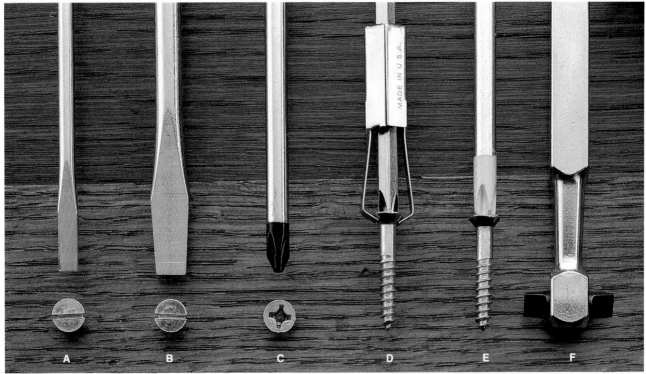

Choose proper screwdriver for the job. Screwdriver tip should fit screw head tightly. (A) Narrow slot screwdriver is too small for this screw head. (B) Wide slot screwdriver is correct for this screw head. (C) Black oxide tip on phillips screwdriver improves control of tool. (D) Screw holder is useful in cramped areas where screw cannot be held by hand. (E) Magnetic screwdriver is useful when driving small screws that are difficult to hold by hand. (F) Offset screwdriver drives screws in cramped spaces.

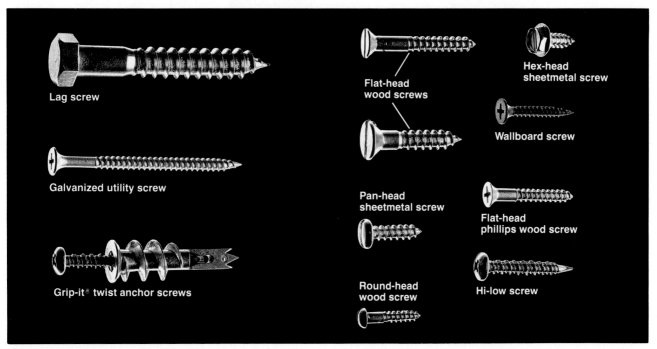

Types of screws: lag screw, galvanized utility screw, Grip-It® twist anchor screws, flat-head wood screws, pan-head sheetmetal screw, oval-head screw, hex-head sheetmetal screw, wallboard screw, flat-head phillips wood screw, hi-low screw.

Screw assortment includes (left to right): flat and oval head wood screws, machine screw with nut, screw with washer for securing fiberglass panels, machine screw, sheetmetal screw, wallboard screw and lag screw.

Select a drill bit slightly smaller than screw shank diameter for drilling a pilot hole.

Pre-bore a pilot hole and countersink the screw head using this combination drill bit.

Lubricate a screw with beeswax for easier driving with a screwdriver or screwgun.

Choose the screwdriver that fits the slot in the screw head. The narrow blade of the driver at right may slip and damage the screw head.

Use a wooden golf tee or dowel to plug oversize screw holes in wood. Cut the plug off flush and drive in a new screw.

Flat or decorative wood buttons are available to cover and conceal countersunk screw heads.

Drive self-tapping sheetmetal screws with an electric screwdriver or electric drill, with a hex socket.

Lubricate screws with beeswax to make driving easier. Do not use soap, oil or grease to lubricate, because they can stain wood and corrode screws.

Pilot hole keeps wood from splitting when screw is driven. Use a twist bit with diameter that is slightly less than diameter of threaded portion of screw.

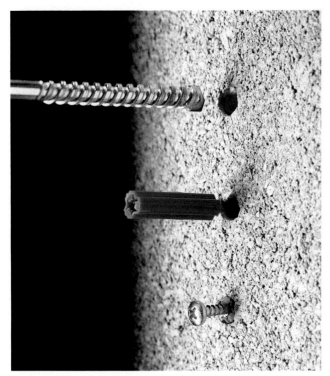

To install a wall anchor, drill a pilot hole in wall equal in diameter to plastic anchor. Insert anchor and drive it flush with wall. Inserted screw will expand anchor for strong, durable hold.

Use finish nail in electric drill to bore a pilot hole in hardwood. Tighten drill chuck securely on nail.

Tooth Guard

Protect handsaw teeth and prevent accidents by covering the cutting edge with a protective sheath when the saw is not in use. A saw sheath can be made from a narrow strip of wood, rigid foam, or old garden hose. Cut a lengthwise slot into one edge of the sheath, then fit it over the saw teeth.

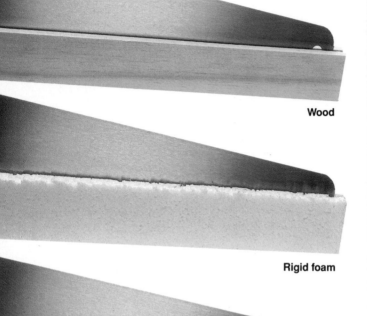

Wood

Rigid foam

Garden hose

Easy Does It

A proper stance is important for good sawing technique. Always take the time to get comfortable before sawing, and make sure your hand, elbow, and shoulder are directly in line with the saw blade. Saw with a steady rhythm, applying slight pressure on the push strokes and relaxing on the pull strokes.

Miss the Mark on Fine Work

A saw consumes from 1/16" to 1/8" of wood because of the thickness of the blade. Sawing directly on a marked cutting line may leave the workpiece slightly too small. Make cuts about 1/16" wide of the marked cutting line. Carefully plane the edge down to the line for a precise fit.

Get the Point

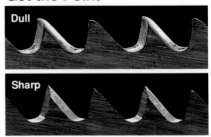

Dull

Sharp

Examine handsaws often for sharpness. On dull saws, the teeth show wear, and are visibly rounded (top). Sharp saws have pointed teeth with clean, smooth edges. Dull saws should be sharpened by a professional. Check the Yellow Pages under "Saws, Sharpening."

Straight Handsaw Cuts

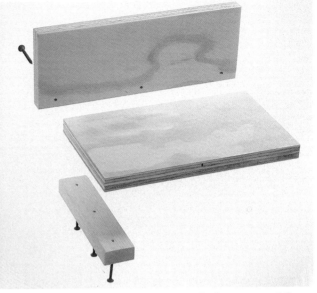

It is important to keep handsaw cuts square to the face and sides of the workpiece. Make this job easier by building a squaring guide from scrap hardwood or ¾" finish plywood. Use a combination square to check each piece for squareness before assembling the guide. Join the pieces with carpenter's glue and 1¼" wallboard screws, and check the final assembly again to make sure it is square.

Adjust Your Sawing Angle

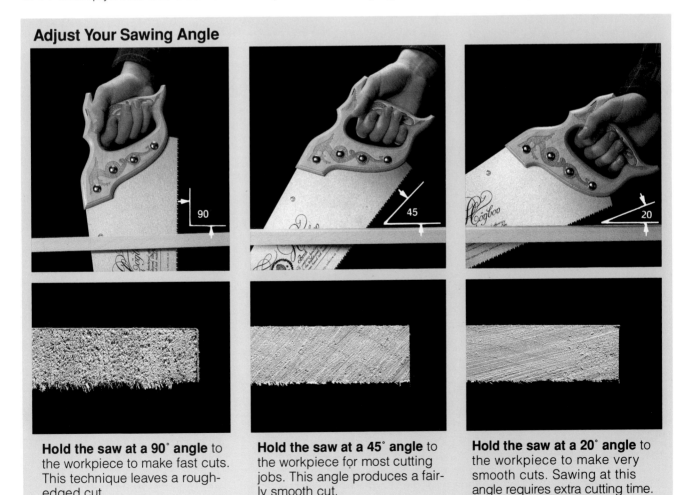

Hold the saw at a 90° angle to the workpiece to make fast cuts. This technique leaves a rough-edged cut.

Hold the saw at a 45° angle to the workpiece for most cutting jobs. This angle produces a fairly smooth cut.

Hold the saw at a 20° angle to the workpiece to make very smooth cuts. Sawing at this angle requires extra cutting time.

Shave and smooth wood with a hand plane. A hand plane has a flat cutting blade set in a steel base and is used to smooth rough surfaces or reduce the width of a piece of wood.

A wood chisel has a flat steel blade set in a handle. It cuts with light hand pressure, or by tapping the end of its handle with a mallet. A wood chisel is often used to cut hinge and lock mortises.

For best results with any shaping tool, make several shallow cuts instead of one deep cut. Forcing a tool to make deep cuts may ruin both the tool and the workpiece.

Before You Start:
Tip: For safety and ease of use, keep shaping tools sharp by honing them on an oilstone or waterstone. Choose a combination stone that has both a coarse and fine face. The stone must be soaked in water or light oil to prevent damage to the tempered metal.

How to Plane a Rough Edge

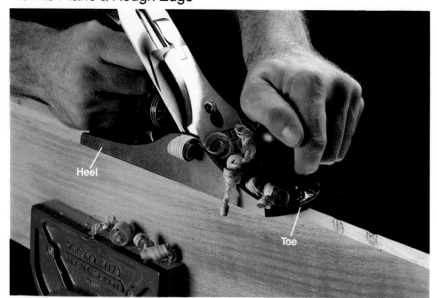

Clamp workpiece into vise. Operate plane so wood grain runs "uphill" ahead of plane. Grip toe knob and handle firmly, and plane with long, smooth strokes. To prevent dipping (overplaning at beginning and end of board), press down on toe of plane at beginning of stroke, and bear down on heel at end of stroke.

How to Chisel a Mortise

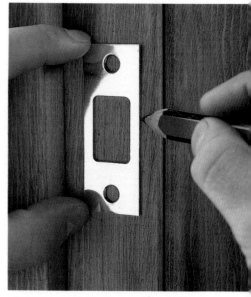

1 Mark outline of mortise with pencil. For strike-plate mortises on door frames, or for hinge mortises, use hardware as marking template when drawing outline.

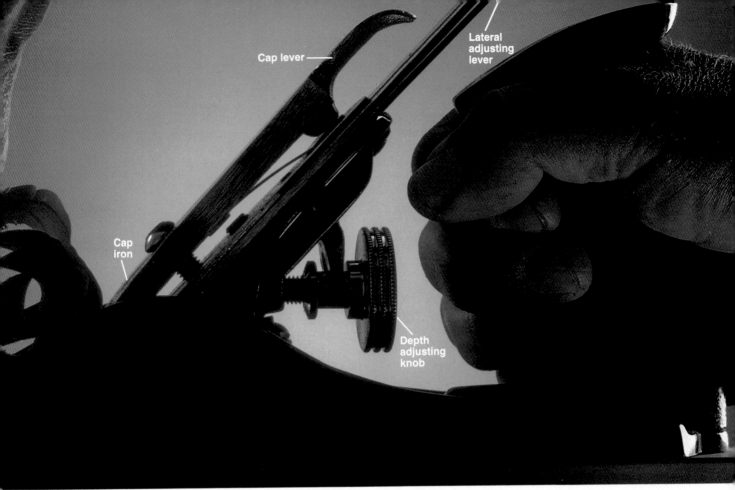

Set plane blade depth with adjusting knob. Properly set cutter will remove wood shavings that are paper-thin. Plane may jam or gouge wood if cutter is set too deep. Use lateral adjusting lever to align cutter for an even cut. If edge of cutter leaves a score mark on wood, check lateral adjustment. Loosen the cap lever to set the cap iron 1/16" back from tip of blade.

2 Cut outline of mortise. Hold chisel with bevel-side in, and tap butt end lightly with mallet until cut is at proper depth.

3 Make a series of parallel depth cuts 1/4" apart across mortise, with chisel held at 45° angle. Drive chisel with light mallet blows to butt end of chisel.

4 Lever out waste chips by holding chisel at a low angle with bevel-side toward work surface. Drive chisel by light hand pressure.

Sharpening Chisels & Plane Blades

It is a good idea to sharpen chisels and planes before each use — even if the tools are brand-new. The factory edges on new blades are sharpened by machine, and are not as sharp as hand-sharpened blades.

Sharpening a tool blade is a two-step process. First, the tool is rough-ground on an electric bench grinder, then it is finish-honed on a fine-grit sharpening stone. If you do not have a

bench grinder, you can use a coarse-grit sharpening stone to rough-grind the blade.

Everything You Need:

Tools: electric bench grinder or coarse-grit sharpening stone, work gloves, fine-grit sharpening stone.

Materials: cup of water, light machine oil.

How to Sharpen Chisels & Plane Blades

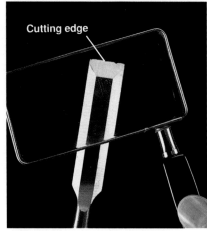

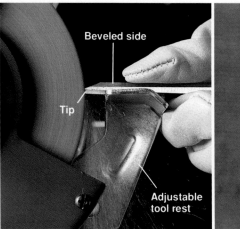

1 Inspect the cutting edge for nicks. Before the blade can be honed on a sharpening stone, any nicks in the steel must be completely removed by grinding.

2 Grind off nicks, using a bench grinder with a medium-grit wheel. Hold the tool on the flat portion of the tool rest, with the beveled side facing up. Hold the tip against the wheel and move it from side to side. Make sure the cutting edge remains square, and cool the blade frequently in water to prevent the metal from losing its temper.

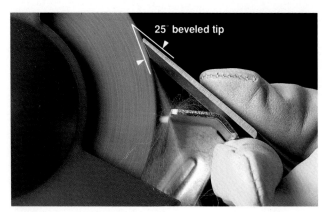

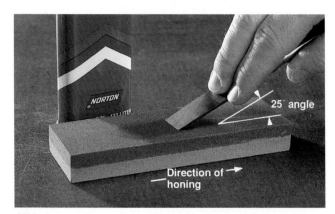

3 Rough-grind the cutting edge by turning the blade so that the beveled side is down. Rest the blade on the angled portion of the tool rest. Move the blade from side to side against the wheel to grind the tip to a 25° bevel, checking often with an angle gauge. Cool the metal frequently in water while grinding.

4 Finish-hone the cutting edge on a fine-grit sharpening stone. Place a few drops of light machine oil on the stone to lubricate the steel and to float away grit and filings. Hold the blade at a 25° angle so the bevel is flat against the stone. Draw it several times across the stone, lifting it away after each pass. Wipe the stone often with a clean rag, and apply oil after each wiping.

How to Sharpen Chisels & Plane Blades (continued)

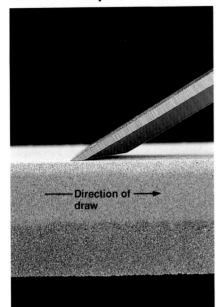

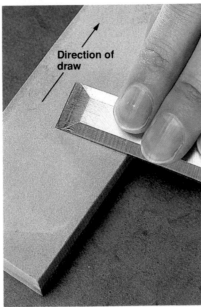

5 Put a "micro-bevel" on the blade by lifting it slightly so only the tip touches the stone. Draw blade two or three times across the stone, until a slight burr can be felt along the back of the blade.

6 Turn the blade over. Holding the blade flat, draw it across the stone one or two times to remove the burr.

7 Examine the cutting edge of the blade. The fine micro-bevel should be about ¹⁄₁₆" wide. This micro-bevel gives the chisel its razor-sharp edge.

Sponge Bath

One way to keep the blade cool when grinding is to hot-glue a piece of sponge to the back of the blade near the cutting edge. Dip the blade in water. The sponge holds water against the back of the blade to draw off heat. When the sponge gets warm, wet it again.

Temper, Temper

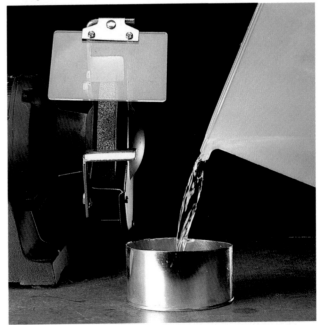

Keep a container of cool water close by when grinding a tool blade. Dip the blade in water frequently to prevent heat from ruining the temper of the steel. When the beads of water on the blade evaporate, it should be dipped again.

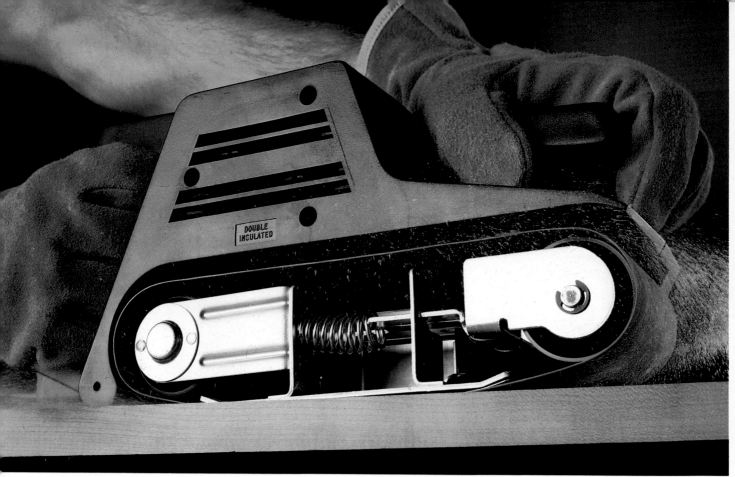

Sand large areas quickly with a belt sander. Disposable belts are available in grits ranging from 36 (extra-coarse) to 100 (fine).

Tools: Sanders

Power sanding tools and sandpaper shape and smooth wood and other building materials. For very large areas, like hardwood floors, use a high-speed floor belt sander. Portable belt sanders are suitable for most work involving rough, fast removal of material. Finishing sanders, sometimes called orbital sanders, are best for light to medium removal of material. For very small, intricate, or contoured areas, sand by hand with folded sandpaper or a sanding block.

Sanders come in several sizes and speed ranges. Small "quarter-sheet" sanders are compact and easy to handle. Larger "half-sheet" sanders are better for sanding large areas. High-speed sanders are best for removing large amounts of material, while lower-speed tools create a fine, smooth finish. Variable-speed sanders offer the greatest flexibility for different applications.

Sandpaper is available in a wide range of grits. The lower the grit number, the coarser the grit. Sanding is usually done in steps, proceeding from coarse-grit sandpaper to finer grits.

Hand sanding block is helpful for small surfaces. For curved areas, wrap sandpaper around a folded piece of scrap carpeting. Sandpaper conforms to shape of workpiece.

60-grit coarse sandpaper is used on hardwood flooring and to grind down badly scratched surfaces. Move sander across the grain for quickest removal.

100-grit medium sandpaper is best used for initial smoothing of wood. Move sander in direction of wood grain for smoothest surface.

150-grit fine sandpaper puts finish smoothness on wood surfaces. Use fine sandpaper to prepare wood surfaces for staining, or to smooth wallboard joints.

220-grit extra-fine sandpaper is used to smooth stained wood before varnishing, or between coats of varnish.

Quality finishing sanders have high-speed motors and orbital action, and can flush-sand in tight work areas. For rough-sanding, move tool across the wood grain. For smooth-finishing, move sander in same direction as wood grain.

Sanding accessories for power drills include (clockwise from top right): disc sander for fast sanding, sanding drums and flap sander to smooth contoured surfaces, and sanding drum on drill attachment.

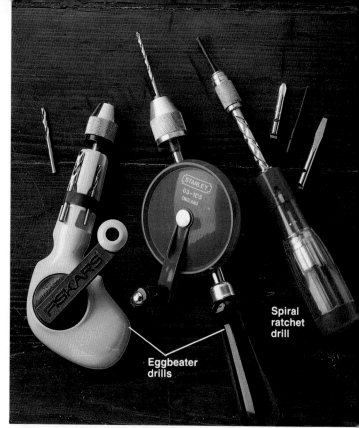

Most drilling jobs can be done easily with a power drill. Power drills are commonly available in ¼-, ⅜- and ½-inch sizes. The number refers to the largest bit shank diameter that fits the drill chuck. A ⅜-inch drill is a good choice because it accepts a wide range of bits and accessories. A variable-speed reversing (VSR) drill will adapt to many uses, like drilling masonry, or driving and removing wallboard screws. A cordless drill offers freedom from extension cords.

When choosing a drill, look for quality features like a 4-amp or larger motor, an extra-long power cord with reinforced cord protector, and a sealed switch that prevents dirt from entering the trigger. A drill that uses top-quality materials may actually be smaller, lighter, and easier to handle than a cheaper drill.

Hand drills include eggbeater and spiral ratchet styles. Hand drills are often used in fine woodworking, or for carpentry jobs where a power drill is not convenient.

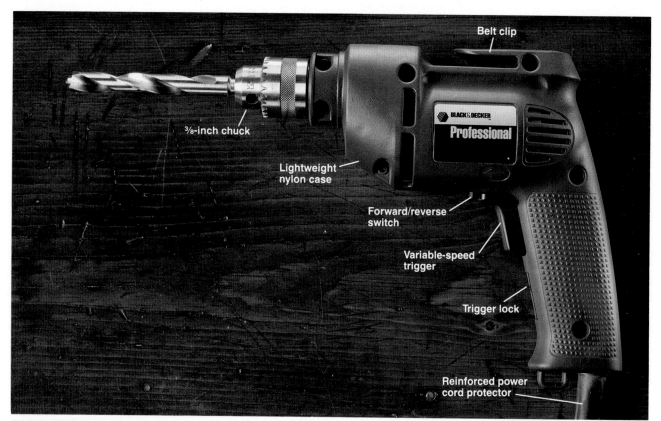

Power drill features to look for include ⅜-inch chuck size, variable motor speed, reversing feature, trigger lock to set a constant speed, a heavy power cord with reinforced protector, a tough lightweight nylon case, and a molded clip that allows the tool to be hung from a belt or pants pocket.

Lubricate metal with cutting oil while drilling. Oil prevents bit from overheating. Use low speed when drilling metal.

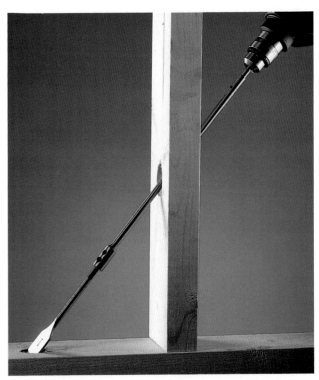

Use bit extension to drill deep or inaccessible holes. Drill at low speed until bit is fully engaged.

Prebore holes in hardwood and metal with a small bit. Preboring prevents bit from binding and wood from splintering.

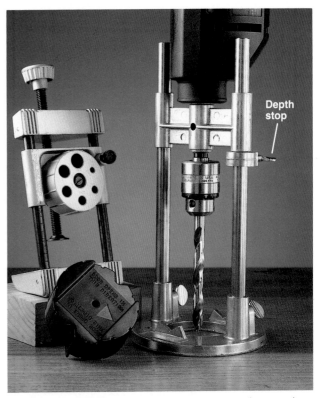

Depth stop

Guide accessories control drilling angles for precise perpendicular holes. Drill guide (right) has adjustable depth stop that controls drilling depth.

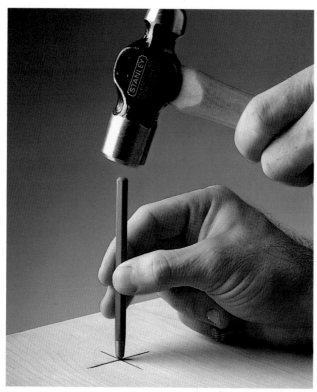

Tap an indentation in wood or metal with a center punch. Starting point keeps drill bit from wandering.

Cover drilling area on glass or ceramic with masking tape. Tape keeps bit from wandering on smooth surface.

Use a backer board underneath workpiece to prevent splintering when drill bit breaks through.

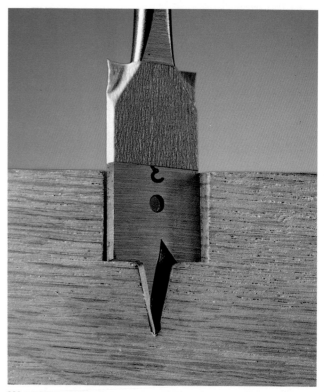

Wrap masking tape around drill bit to control depth of hole. Drill until bottom of tape is even with top of workpiece surface.

How to Sharpen Twist Bits

Sharpen twist bits made of high-speed steel with an electric bit sharpener. Twist bits have precisely curved cutting edges that are impossible to sharpen by hand. Twist bits made from metal alloys, like carbide or titanium, should be sharpened by a professional.

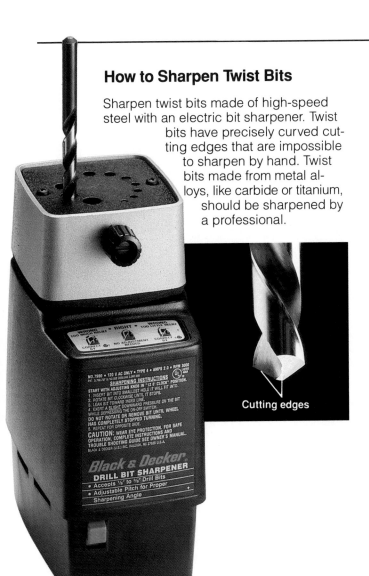

Cutting edges

How to Sharpen Sawtooth Bits

Lifter
Teeth
Throat

Sharpen each tooth with a few light strokes of a triangular saw file, filing in one direction only. Make sure the teeth are equal in height. File the lifter from the inside, passing the file through the throat of the bit.

How to Sharpen Brad-point Bits

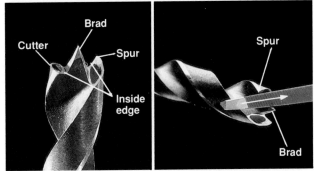

Brad
Cutter
Spur
Inside edge
Spur
Brad

A brad-point bit has a center cutting point called a brad, and a pair of cutters with outside points called spurs. Sharpen the spurs and the inside edges of the cutters with a triangular saw file. Keep the pairs of cutters and spurs at the same height, and take off as little material as possible when sharpening.

How to Sharpen Spade Bits

Wings

1 Clamp the bit securely in the wooden jaws of a bench vise. Grip the wings of the bit in the vise so the bit cannot rotate.

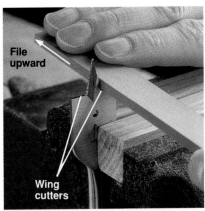

File upward
Wing cutters

2 Sharpen the wing cutters, using a flat metal file. Maintain the angle of the wing cutters, and make a few light strokes, filing upward only. The finished surface should be shiny and smooth.

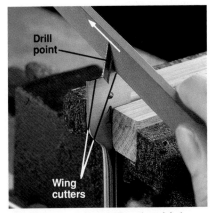

Drill point
Wing cutters

3 Sharpen the drill point. Maintain the angle of the point's cutting edge, and file in one direction only. Keep the file flat against the cutting edge, and avoid touching the wing cutters.

Double-cut Large Timbers

To cut through timbers that are thicker than the maximum blade depth of your circular saw, make matching cuts from opposite sides. Set the blade depth to slightly more than half the thickness of the lumber, and take care to keep the cuts straight.

Getting out of a Bind

Keep your saw from binding in a workpiece by driving a wood shim into the kerf after the cut is started. Keep the kerf open during long cuts by stopping the saw and moving the shim closer to the blade.

Sight Line for Sawing

90°
cutting
line

45
cutting
line

Guiding a circular saw along a cutting line is easier if you draw reference marks on the front of the saw foot with a permanent marker. The cutting path for a bevel cut differs from the path for a 90° cut, so make additional reference marks for common bevel angles, like 45°.

Better Edger

Edge
guide

An edge guide attaches to the foot of your circular saw to help it cut in a straight line. To make the edge guide more stable, attach a straight 8" strip of hardwood to the base of the guide, using pan-head screws.

Take the Plunge

Blade
guard
lever

When making plunge cuts with a circular saw, clamp a 2 × 4 on edge onto the workpiece as a guide. Keep the edge of the saw foot up against the 2 × 4 (inset) when lowering the blade into the workpiece. Use two hands when making plunge cuts, and retract the blade guard before lowering the blade.

Circular Saw Dadoes

You can use your circular saw to cut dadoes and rabbet grooves. Make the outside cuts first, using a crosscut or straightedge guide (pages 30 to 31). Then make several parallel passes between the outside cuts. Clean out the material between the cuts with a wood chisel.

Tip for Ripping

Ripping narrow boards like 2 × 4s can be difficult and dangerous. When making this kind of rip cut, support the foot of the circular saw with another board that is the same thickness as the workpiece.

To keep the boards from sliding as you cut, tack thin strips of wood, like plaster lath, across the bottom of the boards to hold them in place. Make sure tacks are away from the cutting path of the saw.

Maintaining a Circular Saw

For smooth sawing, clean the bottom of the circular saw foot with mineral spirits and a soft cloth after each use. Smooth out any burrs or scratches on the foot with emery cloth. Polish the bottom of the foot with auto paste wax. Clean wood resin from the saw blade with lacquer thinner.

This easy-to-build straightedge guide has a thin plywood base that protects workpiece surfaces and allows for easy positioning and clamping on the workpiece. Keep the metal foot of the circular saw against the cleat when cutting.

Build this Straightedge Guide to Make Long Cuts

Cut sheets of plywood or paneling quickly and accurately with this straightedge guide. Made from two plywood strips, the straightedge guide has a thin base that allows easy positioning on a workpiece. The base also keeps the foot of the circular saw from scratching workpieces.

For accurate cutting, the plywood cleat on the straightedge guide must have a perfectly straight edge. Cut the cleat on a table saw, or use a plywood strip with a factory edge that has been checked for straightness.

This project plan is designed for an 8-ft.-long straightedge guide, but you also may want to make other guides of varying lengths.

Everything You Need:

Tools: tape measure, pencil, C-clamps, circular saw.

Materials: ¼" finish plywood base (10" × 96"), ¾" plywood cleat (2" × 96"), carpenter's glue, sandpaper.

How to Build a Straightedge Guide

1 Apply carpenter's glue to the bottom of the ¾" plywood cleat (A), then position the cleat on the ¼" plywood base (B), 2" from one edge. Clamp the pieces together until the glue dries.

2 Position the circular saw with foot tight against the ¾" plywood cleat. Cut away excess portion of the plywood base with a single pass of the saw. Use sandpaper to smooth any rough edges.

3 To use the straightedge guide, position it with the edge of the base flush against the marked cutting line on the workpiece. Clamp the guide in place with C-clamps.

Build a Triangle Guide for Making Crosscuts & Miters

This triangle guide built from plywood scraps helps you make fast, accurate crosscuts at 90° and 45° angles. You can make additional guides for other common angles, like 30° and 60°.

For a 30°-60° guide, lay out the plywood triangle so that the sides measure exactly 12", 16", and 20". This layout, called a "3-4-5 triangle," gives precise 30°, 60°, and 90° angles.

Everything You Need:

Tools: pencil, combination square, saw.

Materials: ¾" plywood, carpenter's glue, 1¼" wallboard screws, sandpaper.

To use the crosscut guide, hold or clamp the guide so the cleat on the bottom of the guide is tight against the workpiece. Keep the foot of the circular saw firmly against the edge of the plywood triangle while cutting.

How to Make a Triangle Guide

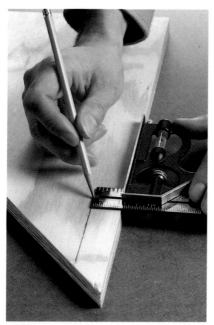

1 Use a combination square to lay out a ¾" plywood triangle with two 45° angles and a 90° angle, and 16" legs. Cut out the triangle. Cut two ¾" plywood cleats, 8" long and 1" wide.

2 Draw a line parallel to one 16" leg of the triangle, 1" from the edge, using a combination square as a guide. Turn the triangle over, and draw an identical line on the other side.

3 Apply carpenter's glue to one side of each plywood cleat. Center the cleats along the edge of the triangle, flush against the reference lines, and attach with wallboard screws. Use sandpaper to smooth rough edges.

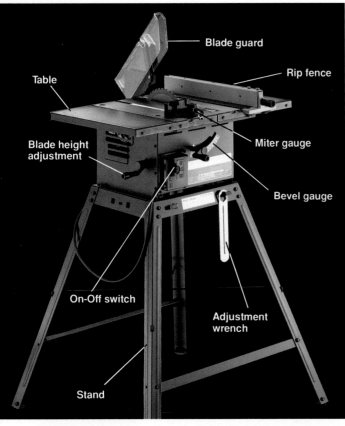

Blade guard

Rip fence

Table

Blade height adjustment

Miter gauge

Bevel gauge

On-Off switch

Adjustment wrench

Stand

The versatile table saw is the first stationary power tool purchased for many home workshops. To keep your table saw cutting safely and accurately, follow these tips:

• Always use the blade guard. Most table saw accidents occur when blade guards are not used. Although many of the photos on the following pages show the table saw with the blade guard removed, this is done for photographic clarity only. Always keep the blade guard in place when sawing.

• Use saw blades designed for the materials you are cutting (see page 38). A blade designed for cutting framing lumber usually is not suitable for fine woodworking.

• Clean away wood pitch, resin, and glue from table saw blades with an old toothbrush and lacquer thinner.

• Make your own table saw accessories to improve safety and increase the usefulness of your saw. Common, easy-to-make accessories include: pushsticks (page 35), fingerboards (pages 36 to 37), and a roller-top support stand.

Shine & Slide

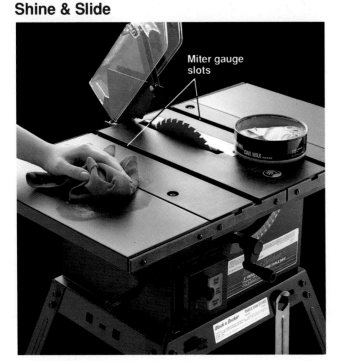

Miter gauge slots

Apply paste wax regularly to the table surface, the sides of the rip fence, and the insides of the miter gauge slots. Buff the surfaces with a soft cloth. The wax prevents rust and helps workpieces slide easily across the table surface.

Keep It Clean

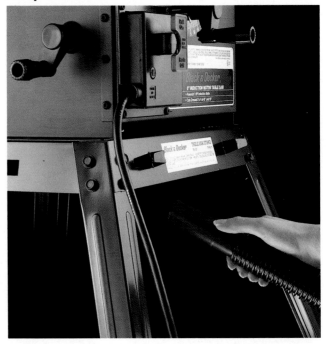

Vacuum inside the motor housing to keep the motor, adjustment screws, and pulleys free of dirt and sawdust. Sawdust buildup can cause malfunctions, such as overheating and binding.

Keep a Low Profile for Safety

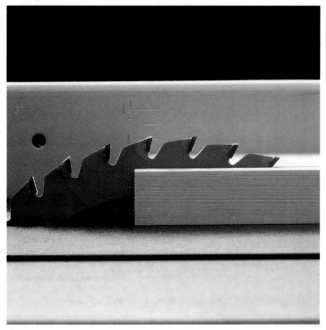

Set the height of the saw blade so it extends no more than ½" above the surface of the workpiece. This minimizes the amount of exposed blade, reducing the chance of touching it accidentally as it spins. A lower blade also reduces blade friction and chipping of workpieces.

Rip Tip

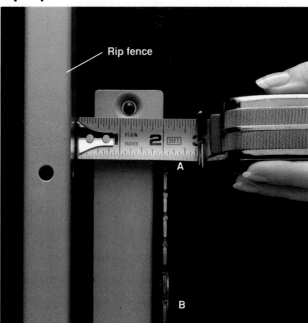

Inaccurate cuts, binding workpieces, and kickbacks are caused by a misaligned saw blade. Check the alignment of the saw blade to the rip fence before each work session. Measure the distance from the rip fence to the blade, both at the front (A) and rear (B) of the blade. Distances should be identical. If they are not, refer to your owner's manual for directions on aligning the saw blade.

Straddle the Fence

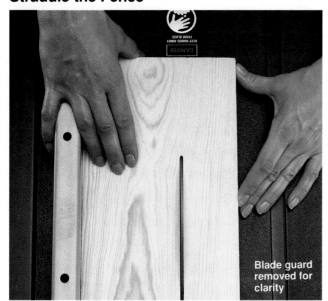

Keep your guide hand away from the blade by hooking the little finger of your hand over the rip fence while cutting. This keeps your hand from slipping off the workpiece and toward the spinning blade.

Cut Big Boards Better

Cut boards that are too wide for the miter gauge in its normal position by turning the miter gauge around so that it precedes the board. Hold the board snugly against the miter gauge, and feed the board slowly into the blade.

How to Check the Vertical Alignment of the Blade

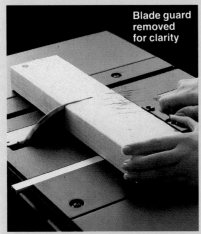

Blade guard removed for clarity

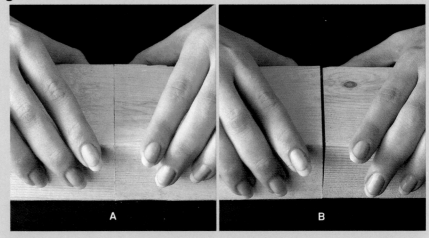

A

B

1 Set both the table saw blade and the miter gauge to 0°. Make a test crosscut on a short length of 2 × 4.

2 Put both pieces of the cut 2 × 4 on a flat surface. Turn one piece upside down, and place the cut ends together. If the ends meet perfectly (A), the blade is exactly vertical. If there is a gap between the two pieces of 2 × 4 (B), then the saw blade is not aligned correctly. Refer to the owner's manual for instructions on how to align the saw blade so it is square to the table.

Put Up a Bigger Fence

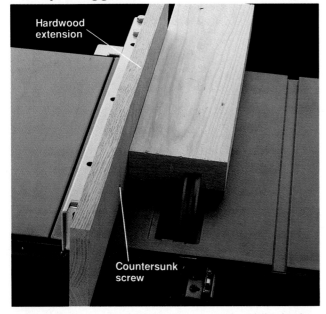

Hardwood extension

Countersunk screw

Long boards are difficult to keep straight while ripping them on the table saw. Solve this problem by attaching a hardwood extension to the rip fence. A larger fence also provides a surface for attaching a fingerboard (pages 36 to 37). The hardwood extension may be any length or height, but the wood must be straight, and free of warping and cupping. Bolt the extension to the rip fence with machine screws and wing nuts, using the mounting holes predrilled on the fence. Make sure to countersink the screw heads so they do not extend past the face of the hardwood.

Miter Mate

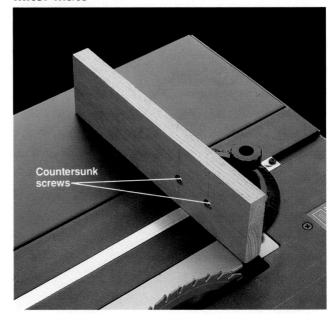

Countersunk screws

Long boards tend to wobble during crosscutting. Solve this problem by attaching a hardwood extension to the miter gauge. The hardwood extension should be straight, and free of warping and cupping. Bolt the extension to the head of the miter gauge with machine screws and wing nuts. Make sure to countersink the screw heads so they do not extend past the face of the hardwood. Make a "right-hand" (above) and "left-hand" extension for easy crosscutting from either side of the blade.

Make a Pushstick for Safety

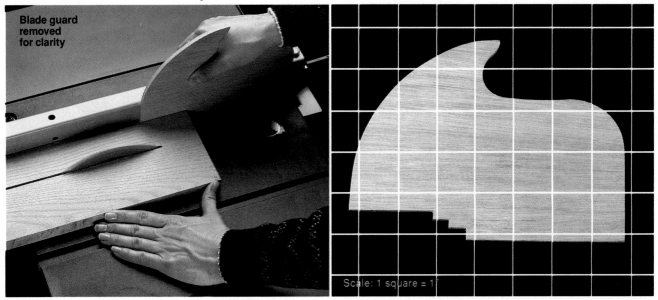

A pushstick is a safety accessory designed to keep your fingers away from the blade as you guide a workpiece across the table saw. This pushstick has several notches to accommodate different thicknesses of wood. The notches grip the back of the workpiece as you press it down against the table and push it forward through the saw blade.

Make the pushstick from plywood dimension lumber free of knots, warping, and other defects. If you wish, make a photocopy transfer (page 56) of the pattern shown above. Make several pushsticks for a variety of ripping tasks. Narrow 1/4" pushsticks are helpful when ripping thin workpieces, but wider pushsticks are more stable.

Straddle Stick Safety

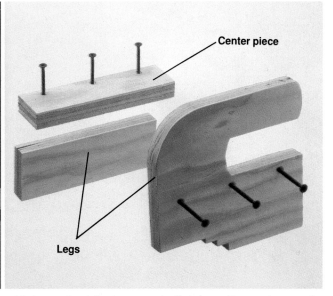

A straddle-type pushstick has two legs that slide on each side of the rip fence. This pushstick is especially stable, preventing the operator's hand from slipping away from the fence and toward the saw blade. The handle of the straddle pushstick should always be over the workpiece. If you are cutting with the rip fence on the left side of the blade, make a "left-hand" pushstick with the handle on the right side.

Make a straddle-type pushstick from three pieces of hardwood or plywood. To prevent wobbling, size the center piece so that the gap between the legs is no more than 1/16" greater than the thickness of the rip fence. The legs ride directly on the table surface, and should be long enough that the center piece clears any adjustment bolt heads on top of the rip fence. Join the pieces with wallboard screws.

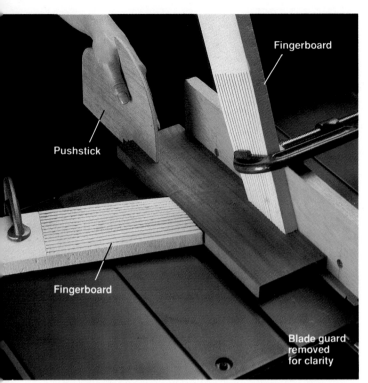

Two fingerboards clamped against the saw table and rip fence are especially helpful for making dadoes or precise cuts on hardwoods.

Use Fingerboards for Safe, Accurate Cutting

A fingerboard is an easy-to-make table saw accessory that is clamped to the rip fence or saw table to help guide a workpiece while cutting. It has springlike fingers that apply steady pressure as the workpiece is fed through the saw blade. Fingerboards are especially useful in fine woodworking projects, where the slightest error can ruin a workpiece.

Using fingerboards improves saw safety. When used properly, fingerboards reduce the chance of kickbacks; they also keep the operator's hands well away from the saw blade. When cutting narrow workpieces, use a pushstick in addition to fingerboards.

Everything You Need:

Tools: pencil, combination square, jig saw with wood-cutting blade, C-clamp.

Materials: straight-grained 1 × 4 pine lumber (about 12" long).

How to Make & Use a Fingerboard

1 Select a piece of straight-grained 1 × 4 pine lumber. The board must be free of knots, checks, or splits. Use a combination square to mark a stop line 8" from the end of the board.

2 Mark a series of parallel lines, ¼" apart, from the long end of the board to the stop line.

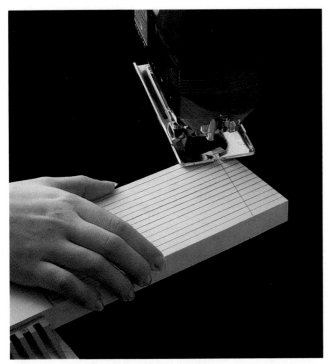

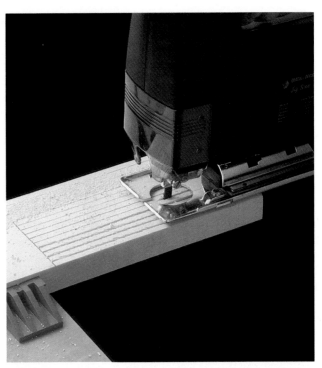

3 Make sure the wood is clamped securely on a workbench or portable work station with the marked portion overhanging the edge of the work surface. Mark the end of the board at a 20° angle, then trim off the end, using a jig saw.

4 Make a series of parallel cuts from the end of the board to the stop line, following the marked lines carefully. Stop the jig saw at the end of each cut, and allow the blade to come to a complete halt before removing it.

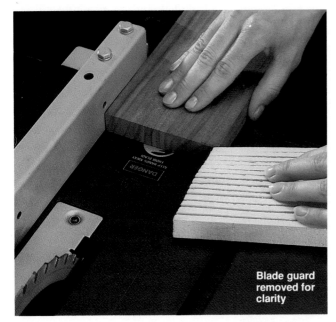

Blade guard removed for clarity

Blade guard removed for clarity

5 To use the fingerboard, place the workpiece on the saw table, about 4" in front of the blade. Position the fingerboard at an angle, slightly blocking the front corner of the workpiece. Clamp the fingerboard to the saw table with a C-clamp or handscrew. The fingerboard should be positioned so force is applied against the rip fence, not against the saw blade.

6 Turn on the saw. Feed the workpiece into the blade with steady hand pressure. The fingerboard "fingers" should flex slightly as the workpiece travels forward. Use a pushstick (page 35) to guide the workpiece past the fingerboard.

Mighty Miter Maker

The power miter saw is a versatile, portable tool that is especially useful for finish carpentry and woodworking projects.

When using a power miter saw, anchor it firmly with C-clamps to a workbench or portable work station. Reduce vibrations and tool noise by placing pads cut from an inner tube or carpet padding between the saw legs and the work surface. Prevent rust from forming on the saw bed by polishing it with auto paste wax.

Many shop workers increase the size of the metal saw bed by attaching a layer of ¾" particleboard or plywood over the bed. The oversized wood layer protects the metal bed and provides extra support when cutting long boards.

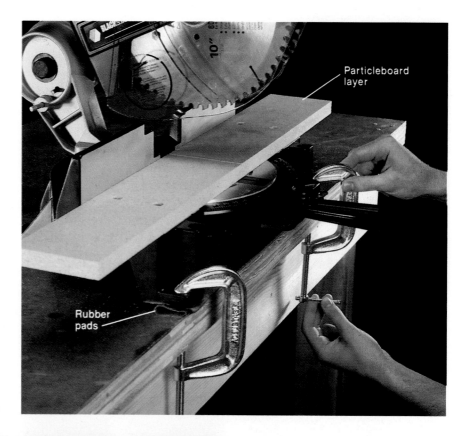

Particleboard layer

Rubber pads

On the Cutting Edge

The quality of the cut produced by a power saw depends on the type of blade you use and the speed at which the blade is forced through the workpiece. In general, let the saw motor reach full speed before cutting, and lower the saw arm slowly for the best results.

A 16-tooth carbide-tipped blade (A) cuts quickly: it is good for rough cutting of framing lumber.

A 60-tooth carbide-tipped blade (B) makes a smooth cut in both softwoods and hardwoods. It is a good all-purpose blade for general shop work.

A precision-ground crosscut and miter blade (C) makes extremely smooth, splinter-free cuts. It is an ideal blade for your fine woodworking projects.

An abrasive friction blade (D) makes fast cuts on thin steel, galvanized metals, and iron pipes.

A

B

C

D

Keep It under Lock & Key

Prevent unauthorized use of a miter saw by locking it with a small luggage padlock placed through the hole in the trigger.

Easy Angle Finder

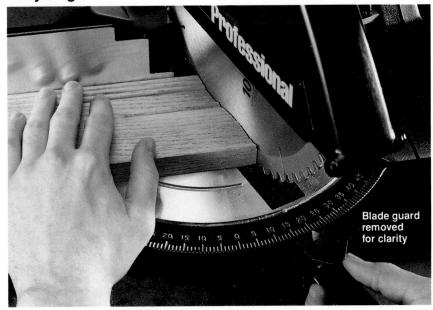

Blade guard removed for clarity

Use your miter saw as a protractor to find the angle of mitered workpieces. Lock the saw blade in the down position, then place the workpiece on the miter saw table, tight against the rear fence. Adjust the saw arm until the blade is tight against the angled portion of the workpiece. Read the miter scale to find the angle of the workpiece.

Crowning Touch

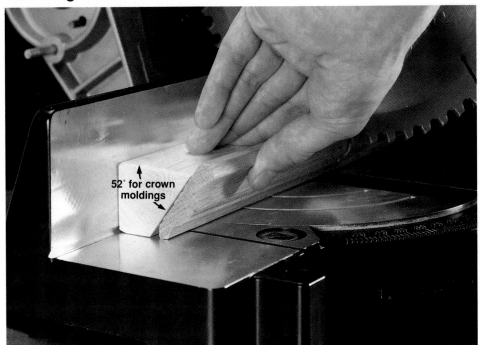

52° for crown moldings

Crown and cove moldings do not lie flat on the wall when installed. For this reason, it is difficult to miter them accurately. To make this job easier, attach a beveled spacer block to the miter saw fence to duplicate the angle at which the molding will be installed. For crown moldings, bevel the spacer block at 52°; for cove moldings, bevel the block at 45°. Drill holes through the rear of the fence, and attach the block to the fence with pan-head screws.

A Square Deal

Correct blade alignment is essential for accurate mitering. Over time, a miter saw can lose its alignment. Before each job, check the alignment between the blade and the saw table, using a carpenter's square or the blade alignment test described on page 34. Realign the blade according to the directions in your owner's manual. Most power miter saws have handle bolts underneath the saw table that can be loosened to re-adjust the alignment of the blade.

Blade guard removed for clarity

Maximum Mitering

A standard miter saw with a 10" blade makes a cut 5¼" long with the blade set at 90°, and 4" long with the blade set at 45°. You can cut through wider boards by placing a 2 × 4 block on the saw table. The block raises the workpiece so more of the saw blade cuts into it. With the block, the maximum cut is 6¼" at 90°, and 4½" at 45°.

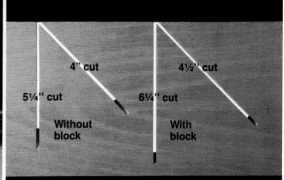

4" cut

4½" cut

5¼" cut

6¼" cut

Without block

With block

How to Cut Extra-wide Boards

Blade guard removed for clarity

1 Make a full downward cut. Raise the saw arm, release the trigger, and let the saw blade come to a full stop.

Blade guard removed for clarity

2 Turn the workpiece over, and carefully align the first cut with the saw blade. Make a second downward cut to finish the job.

Perfect Plastic Pipe Cutter

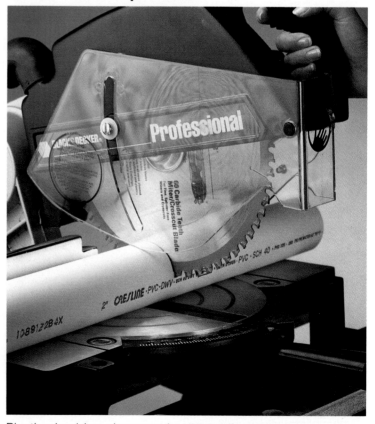

Plastic plumbing pipes can be cut easily on the power miter saw, using any type of blade. When cutting metal plumbing pipes, use an abrasive friction blade (page 38).

Prevent Kickbacks with a Miter Stop Block

When cutting many workpieces to the same length, some shop workers clamp a block of wood, called a "stop block," to the rear fence of the miter saw. They butt the workpieces against the stop block before cutting to ensure that the pieces are cut to the same size. But using a solid block of wood as a stop block can be dangerous. Small pieces of wood can jam between the saw blade and the clamped block, causing kickbacks that may injure the operator.

Avoid this danger by making this flip-out stop block from scrap 1" lumber. Size the stop block to fit your saw fence, and assemble the pieces (exploded view, right) with wire brads and carpenter's glue.

Everything You Need:

Tools: saw, screwdriver, C-clamp.

Materials: scrap 1" lumber, wire brads, carpenter's glue, 1½" × 2" hinge with screws, screw eye.

How to Use a Miter Stop Block

1 Clamp the stop block against the rear fence of the saw at the desired position, using a C-clamp. Position the workpiece on the saw bed so it butts against the stop block.

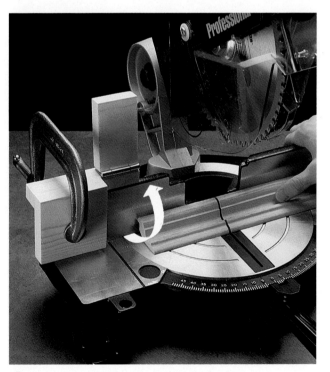

2 Hold the workpiece in place, then flip the hinged portion of the stop block out of the way. Cut the workpiece, then let the saw come to a complete stop before flipping the stop block down and cutting additional workpieces.

Cut decorative shapes, make grooves, and trim laminates with a router. A router is a high-speed power tool that uses changeable bits to perform a variety of cutting and shaping tasks. Because a router runs at speeds up to 25,000 revolutions per minute, it can make very smooth cuts in even the hardest woods.

For best results, make a series of routing passes, gradually extending the bit until cut reaches the correct depth. Experiment to find the proper speed for moving the router. Pushing the tool too fast slows the motor, causing the wood to chip and splinter. Moving it too slowly can scorch the wood.

Choose a router with a motor rated at 1 horsepower or more. Safety features may include a conveniently placed ON/OFF trigger switch, clear plastic chip guard, and a built-in work light.

Tip: Router bits spin in a clockwise direction, so the tool has a tendency to drift to the left. For best control, feed the router from left to right so that the cutting edge of the bit feeds into the wood.

Decorative edging is usually made with a bit that has a pilot at the tip. The round pilot rides against the edge of the workpiece to control the cut.

Corner rounding bit makes simple finish edges on furniture and wood moldings.

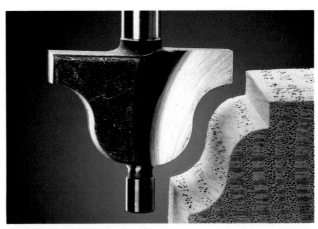

Ogee bit cuts a traditional, decorative shape in wood. Ogee bits are often used to create wood moldings and to shape the edges of furniture components.

Rabbet bit makes step-cut edges. Rabbeted edges are often used for woodworking joints and for picture frame moldings.

Laminate trimmer bit cuts a finished edge on plastic laminate installations. Ball-bearing pilot prevents bit from scorching face of laminate.

Straight bit cuts a square, flat-bottomed groove. Use it to make woodworking joints, or for free-hand routing.

Dovetail bit cuts wedge-shaped grooves used to make interlocking joints for furniture construction and cabinetwork.

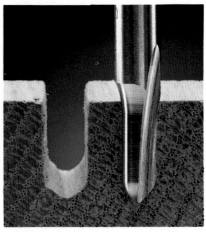

Veining bit is a round-bottomed cutter used for free-hand decorative carving and lettering.

Going around in Circles

Cut circles easily with a router, using a screw and a short length of chain. Drive the screw in the center point of the circle, then attach the end of the chain to the screw. Attach the other end of the chain to the router handle. To cut the circle, stretch the chain taut against the screw, then lower the bit into the workpiece and move the router slowly around the center point of the circle.

Stop Router Wobble

When you are cutting a decorative edge, the slightest wobble can ruin the workpiece. Keep the router base flat by clamping a piece of scrap lumber the same thickness as the workpiece to the surface of the workbench.

Homemade Router Tool

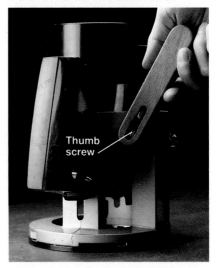

Thumb screw

Motor vibrations can tighten a router base thumbscrew so it is difficult to loosen. Make a hardwood router wrench to help loosen a stubborn thumbscrew. Cut a 1" × 5" strip of ¾" hardwood, then cut a narrow slot near one end, just large enough to slip over the thumbscrew.

Stay on Edge

Keep your router from wobbling when cutting edge grooves by clamping scrap lumber to both sides of the workpiece, flush with the top edge. The scrap wood also provides a surface for a router straight guide to run against.

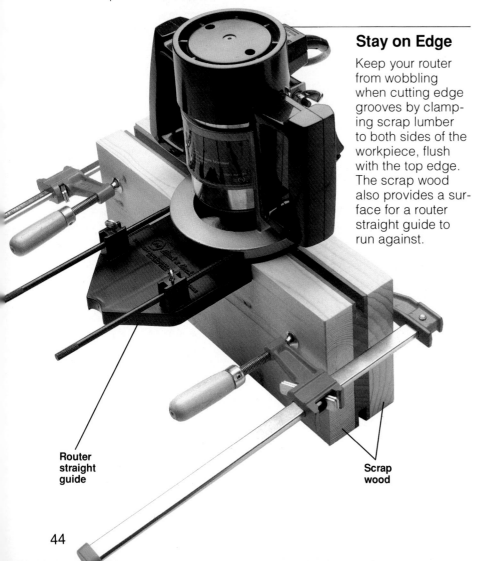

Router straight guide

Scrap wood

Build a Router T-square for Quick, Accurate Cuts

This T-square makes it easy to cut straight grooves (dadoes) with a router. It has precut reference slots that make it easy to position the T-square accurately on the workpiece.

This plan is for a T-square with ½" and ¾" reference slots. You also can make the reference slots to match other frequently used bit sizes. If you wish, make a larger T-square for cutting grooves in sheet goods.

Everything You Need:

Tools: combination square, screwdriver, clamp, router, router bits (straight ½", ¾").

Materials: ½" plywood (3" × 18"), 2 × 4 (14" long), 1⅝" wallboard screws.

To use the router T-square, clamp it on the workpiece so the reference slot aligns with dado layout mark on the workpiece. Keep router firmly against the T-square guide arm to ensure a perfect cut.

How to Make & Use a Router T-square

1 Center one end of the guide arm (A) on the cross bar (B), so it overhangs the cross bar by 4". Use a combination square to make sure the pieces are exactly perpendicular.

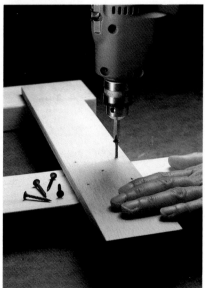

2 Attach the guide arm to the cross bar with wallboard screws. After driving the first screw, check to make sure the pieces are perpendicular, then drive the remaining screws.

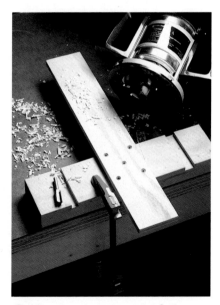

3 Use your router and a ¾" straight bit to cut a ½"-deep reference slot in one side of the cross bar. Cut another slot on the other side of the cross bar, using a ½" straight bit.

Hammer drill combines impact action with rotary motion for quick boring in concrete and masonry. To minimize dust and to keep bits from overheating, lubricate the drill site with water. A hammer drill can also be used for conventional drilling when the motor is set for rotary action only.

Air-powered nailer or stapler is attached to an air compressor. Tool trigger releases a burst of air to drive nails or staples into wood.

Reciprocating saw can be used for making cutouts in walls or floors, where a circular saw will not work, or for cutting metals like cast-iron plumbing pipes.

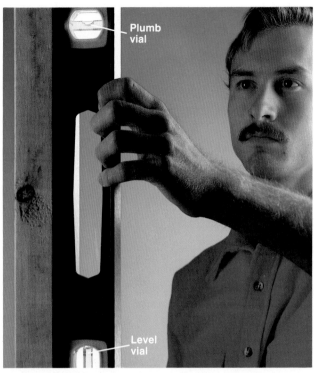

Two-foot carpenter's level has plumb vial for checking vertical surfaces and a level vial for checking horizontal surfaces. Level shows correct position when bubble is exactly between the line markings.

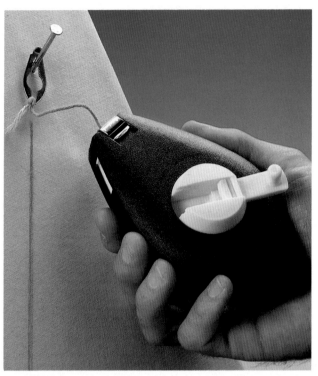

Chalk line marks long lines needed for large layout jobs. Hold string taut at both ends, and snap firmly to mark surface. Chalk line can also be used as a plumb bob for laying out stud walls.

How to Duplicate Angles with a T-bevel

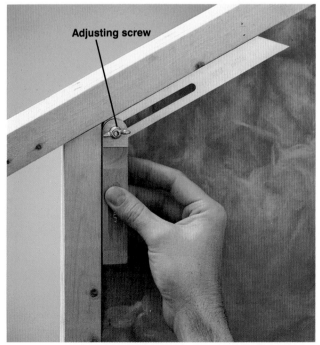

1 Loosen the T-bevel adjusting screw and adjust the arms to match the angle to be copied. Tighten the adjusting screw.

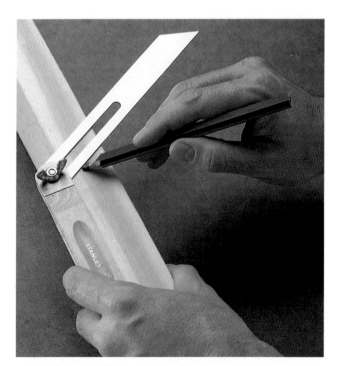

2 Move the T-bevel to the workpiece, and mark the profile of the angle. Cut the workpiece to match the angle.

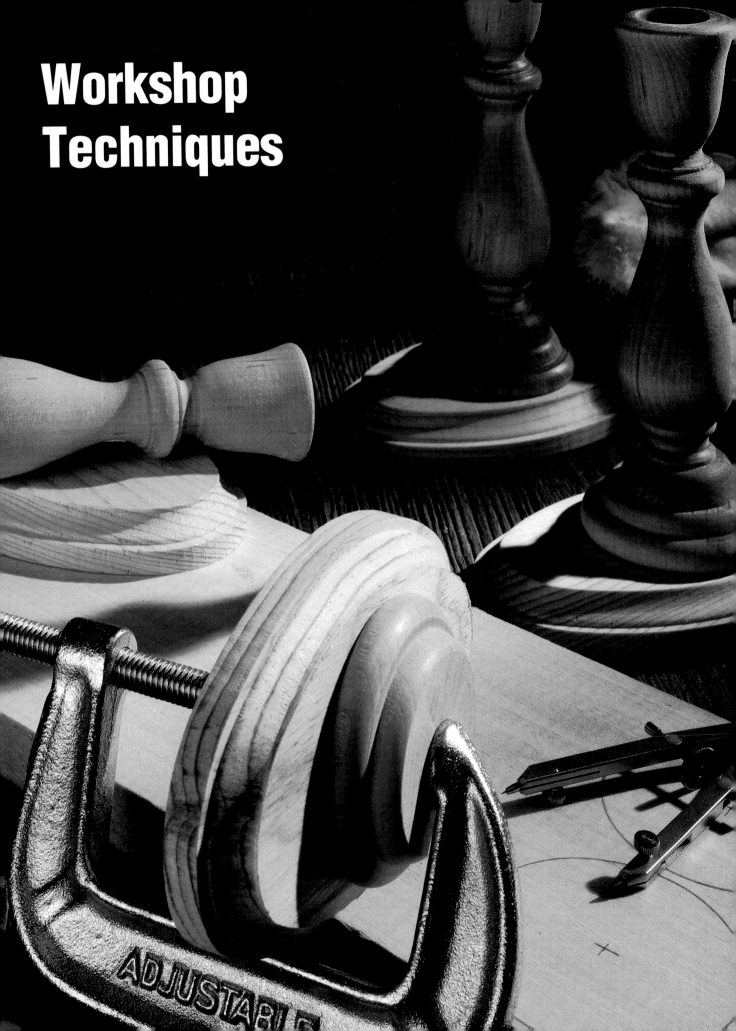

Workshop Techniques

Using good tools and materials is just part of what goes into making a successful project. In particular, the basic techniques used to begin and complete a project affect its attractiveness, and the ease and accuracy of your work.

This section presents dozens of tips and innovations that will help you improve these techniques. Not only will these tips give you better results, they will save you time and money.

Included are tips that help you begin a project with precise patterns, and show you more accurate measuring methods. Other tips show you more effective clamping techniques, and how to get the best use from adhesives. Finally, there are more tips for sanding your projects, including a number of jigs for sanding contours.

Standard Circles

A piece of shelving standard makes a quick and versatile compass. Drive a nail through the screw hole at one end of the standard and into the workpiece to mark the center of the circle. Place the pencil in one of the slots so that the distance between the nail and the pencil is equal to the radius of the circle. Rotate the standard around the nail to draw the circle.

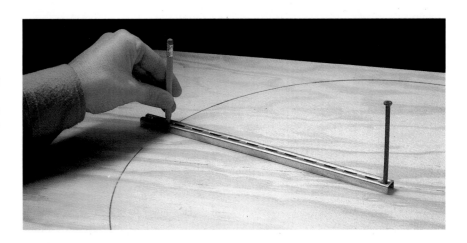

Quick Rough-cut Marking

Use your finger and a pencil to make quick, "close-enough" marks for rough cuts. Hold the pencil between your thumb and forefinger as shown. The width you wish to mark determines how far from the tip you must hold the pencil. Brace the last three fingers against the edge of the board and use them to guide the pencil as you pull it toward you.

Separate & Not Equal

Different tape measures do not always measure equally. A slight difference in the end hooks can create an error of 1/16" or more between two tapes, even if they are the same brand and style. If possible, use only one tape measure while working on a project. If you must work with two tapes, check them to make sure they record the same measurement.

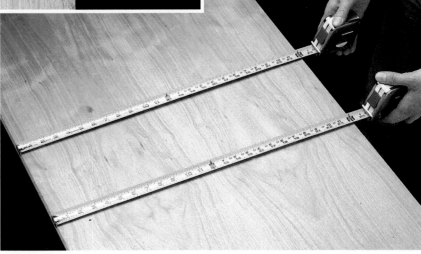

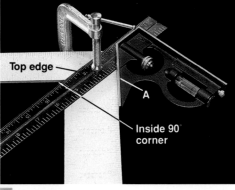

Top edge

A

Inside 90°
corner

Bull's-eye

Find the center of a round or cylindrical workpiece with this jig. Clamp a combination square onto a framing square (above) so that the 45° face of the combination square (A) rests against one leg of the framing square. The top edge of the combination square should intersect the inside 90° corner of the framing square.

Place the jig over the workpiece so both legs of the framing square touch the edges of the workpiece, as shown (left). Draw a pencil line along the top edge of the combination square blade. Rotate the workpiece several times and mark additional lines. The center of the workpiece is the point where the lines intersect.

Accurate Inside Measurements

Taking an accurate inside measurement of a drawer or box is difficult because a tape measure blade will not fit into a corner (left). The measurement on the tape measure case that indicates its length is not accurate enough for precise work. For accurate measurements, position a square in the bottom of the workpiece, tight against the corner (below). Use a tape measure to measure from the opposite side of the workpiece to the tip of the square. Add the length of the square blade (A) to the tape measurement (B) to find the total inside measurement.

B — A —

Skip the Hook

The end hook on a tape measure has a small amount of play in it, and should not be used when an extremely accurate measurement is needed. For precise measurements, use the 1" mark as a beginning point. Remember to subtract 1" from the final reading.

Large Circle Compass

You can make a simple compass for marking large circles using a 2"-wide strip of ½"-thick plywood. Cut the strip 2" longer than the radius of the circle. Drill a ¼" hole in the center of the strip, 1" from one end. At the other end, drill a 5/16" hole in the center of the strip, 1" from the end. Push the point of an awl through the ¼" hole and into the workpiece at the center of the circle. Insert a pencil into the 5/16" hole, and keeping the pencil straight up and down, rotate the strip around the awl to mark the circle.

Long Division

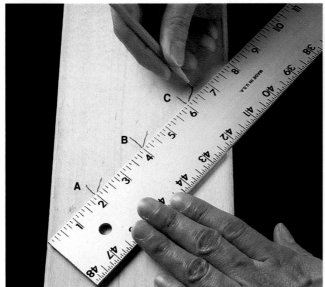

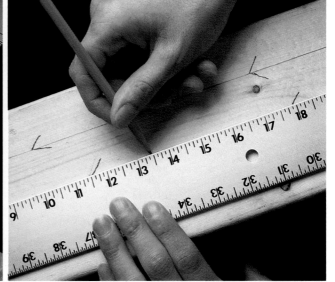

Dividing a board lengthwise into equal strips is difficult if the width of the board is not easily divisible by the number of parts. For example, you want to cut a 5¾"-wide board into 4 equal strips. To do this job quickly and easily, position the 0" end of a ruler at one edge of the board. Angle the ruler across the board until the opposite edge of the board touches an inch measurement that is easily divisible by the number of parts. For the example above, the ruler is angled until the 8" mark touches the edge of the board, and 8" divided by 4 equals 2". Mark the board at this interval along the ruler (A, B, C). Repeat this procedure at another location on the board, then use the marks to draw parallel cutting lines on the board.

Multi-digital Leveling

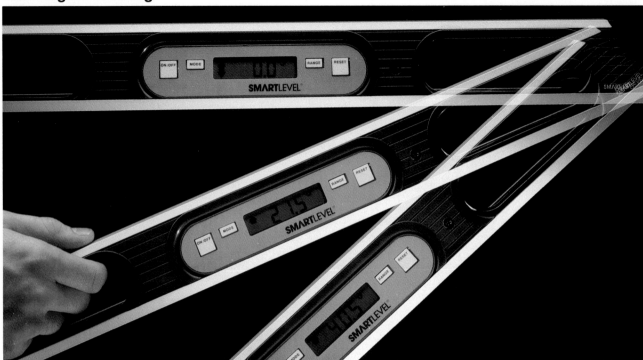

Electronic levels are new tools providing very accurate angle readings with digital readouts instead of bubble gauges. They will also measure pitch and slope percentages automatically. Powered by a replaceable battery, electronic levels are very durable and are easy to recalibrate. The electronic components are contained in a module that can be used alone as a torpedo level, or inserted into frames of varying lengths.

Is Your Level on the Level?

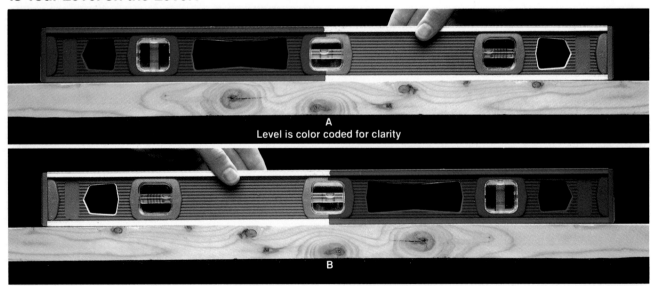

A
Level is color coded for clarity

B

Check a level frequently to ensure that it reads correctly. Before buying a new level, check to make sure it is accurate. To check a level for accuracy, hold one side of the level against an even surface (A), and read the bubble gauge carefully, noting exactly where the bubble is located against the guidelines. Turn the level 180° (B) and read the gauge again. Next, turn the level upside down and read the gauge. The bubble should be in the same position for all three readings. If not, use the mounting screws to adjust the bubble gauges until the level reads accurately. Gauges that are cracked should be replaced. If the gauges cannot be adjusted or replaced, buy a new level.

Sound Out Your Room

A sonic measuring tool, available at home centers, is a quick method for determining room size. This tool measures distance by bouncing sound waves off of hard surfaces, and units are available that will measure up to 250 feet with 99.5 percent accuracy. The tool also has a built-in calculator for adding distances and computing area and volume measurements. Temperature changes can affect the tool's accuracy, so let it adjust to room temperature for 15 minutes before using it.

Quick Check for Square

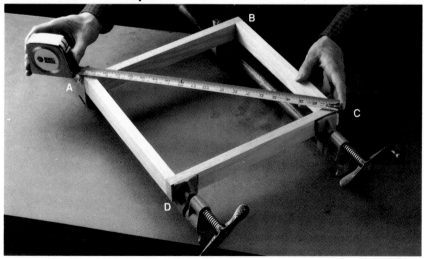

Checking for square is crucial when building frames, boxes, cabinets, drawers, and other projects where fit is important. To check for square quickly, measure the diagonals of the workpiece (A-C, B-D). The measurements will be identical if the workpiece is square.

Leveling Around Warps

Dimension lumber with slight warps and bows is usable, but checking the boards for plumb or level is difficult. Make a leveling jig for warped lumber by cutting a straightedge on a table saw, and attaching short 2 × 4 blocks to the ends. The straightedge should be slightly shorter than the lumber you are checking. Tape or clamp a level to the straightedge on the side opposite the 2 × 4 blocks. Hold the straightedge against the lumber and read the level to check for plumb or level. You can straighten the warp or bow with a cripple.

Quick Draw

To draw a line parallel to the edge of a board quickly, set the blade of a combination square to the desired distance. Position the flat side of the square against the edge of the board, and place a pencil at the end of the blade. Pull the square and pencil toward you to draw the line.

Tracing Tool

A pattern tracing wheel used in sewing also can be used to copy patterns in the workshop. Tape your pattern onto the workpiece, then follow the lines with the pattern wheel, applying downward pressure to the tool. The serrated edge of the wheel will leave marks to follow when cutting out the workpiece.

Story Pole

When marking an identical series of measurements on many workpieces, save time and improve accuracy by creating a marking pattern, called a story pole. Make the story pole from a piece of scrap lumber. Carefully mark the measurements on the story pole, then use it as a template for marking the workpieces instead of taking individual measurements.

Story pole

PATTERN "A"

Repetitive Cuts

When you are cutting a series of identical workpieces, use only one piece as the pattern for laying out the other pieces. If you use each new piece to lay out the next piece, each new piece will be slightly larger than the last.

Diameter Gauge

To measure the diameter of round workpieces easily, make a simple gauge with a ruler and two squared blocks of wood. To find the diameter, place the workpiece between the two wood blocks and the ruler as shown. The diameter measurement is then read on the ruler. For this gauge to work properly, all six faces of each wood block must be squared.

Pattern Rubbing

To make a pattern of an object or shape that cannot be traced or photocopied, lay a sheet of white paper over the original. Rub the paper with your fingers until the features of the original make an impression in the paper. Cut out this pattern or transfer it to the workpiece with a pattern tracing wheel (page opposite).

Board Center Marker

Find and mark the center of your workpieces quickly with this simple marking jig. Make it from 2 x 4 stock and 5/16" doweling. On one side of the gauge shown here the dowels are centered 1" on either side of the pencil hole. Make sure the distance between each dowel and the pencil hole is equal. This side is used for marking center on pieces up to 1 5/8" wide. The other side has the dowels centered 4 1/8" on each side of the pencil hole, and is used on boards up to 7 3/4" wide. If you often use wider stock, you may wish to make a larger gauge.

The pattern lines from a photocopy can be transferred to a workpiece using a hot iron. It may take two or three passes with the iron to completely transfer the pattern.

Photocopy Pattern Transfer

To transfer a project pattern to a workpiece quickly and accurately, make a photocopy of the pattern and use an iron to transfer the outline to the workpiece. To make enlarged or reduced patterns, use a copying machine that has a zoom feature.

If the pattern includes any lettering, the image must be reversed before it can be transferred to the workpiece. To reverse the pattern, first make a photocopy on transparent tissue paper. Next, position the tissue copy on the photocopy machine so that the image is face up, and make a second photocopy. The second copy will have a reversed image that will transfer correctly to the workpiece.

Everything You Need:

Tools: copy machine, iron.

Materials: masking tape.

How to Make a Photocopy Pattern Transfer

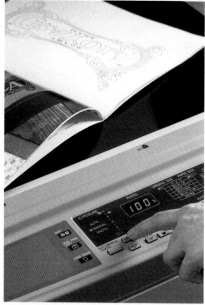

1 Make a photocopy of the pattern. If possible, set the copy machine to make a dark copy. This will make transferring the copy easier.

2 Position the copy on the workpiece. Tape the copy in place, taping along one edge only.

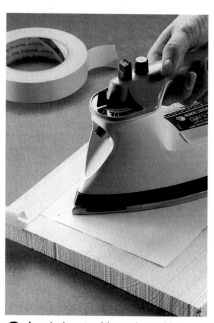

3 Apply heat with an iron. Keep the iron moving to avoid scorching the pattern. Periodically lift the paper to check for areas that need more heat.

Contact Paper Pattern

Protect workpiece surfaces from pencil marks and scratches by covering the workpiece with clear contact paper before marking the cutting pattern. Contact paper works well on hard-to-mark surfaces, like metal and glass. Leave the paper in place until all cutting is completed.

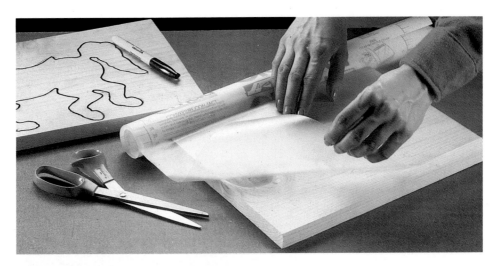

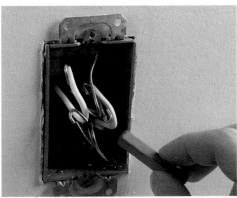

Tape Drawing Surface

Some materials, like plastic, glass, ceramics, and metals, are difficult to mark. Solve this problem by using artist's tape to provide a surface on which to draw the pattern lines. Leave the tape in place until you are finished cutting. Artist's tape is easy to remove, and can be purchased at stationery stores or art supply shops.

Marking Protrusions

Cutting around protrusions like electrical boxes can be difficult when installing paneling or other sheet goods. Simplify this job by coating the edges of the box with carpenter's chalk. Press the back side of the paneling against the box to transfer the chalk outline. Cut out the outline with a jig saw.

Handscrews are wooden clamps with two adjusting screws. Handscrews are used to hold materials together while gluing. The wide wooden jaws will not damage workpiece surfaces. Handscrews adjust to fit angled workpieces.

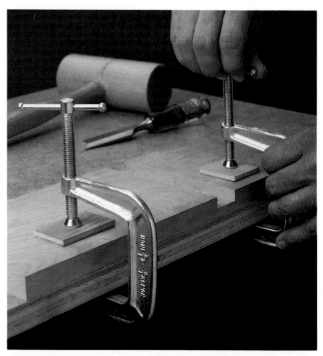

C-clamps range in clamping capacity from 1 to 6". To protect the workpiece, place scrap wood blocks between the jaws and the workpiece surface.

Corner clamp holds mitered corners when gluing picture frame moldings. Glue and clamp opposite corners, and let them dry before gluing the remaining corners.

Three-way clamp has three thumbscrews, and is used to hold edge moldings to the side of a shelf, tabletop or other flat surface. Use scraps of wood to protect workpiece surfaces.

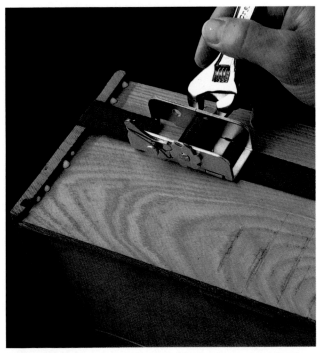

Strap clamp and white carpenter's glue are used for gluing furniture and other wood projects. Use yellow glue for exterior projects. Clamp the pieces together until the glue dries.

Pipe clamps or bar clamps hold large workpieces. Buy pipe clamp jaws in pairs to fit either ½-inch or ¾-inch diameter pipe. Clamping irregular shapes may require clamping jigs made from scrap lumber.

Workmate® portable gripping bench has a jointed, adjustable table that tightens to clamp a workpiece. Accessories, like bench stops, increase the gripping bench's versatility.

Vise-Grip® clamps provide good holding power and are easily adjusted. The hand-grip closing action makes these clamps quicker to use than traditional C-clamps.

Sawhorse Stirrup

Long workpieces balanced on a pair of sawhorses can be difficult to hold in place. Hold them securely with a bicycle inner tube. Slide the inner tube over the workpiece, and use your foot to stretch the inner tube and hold the lumber in place while you work.

Rubber Band Clamp

Use a bicycle inner tube to hold chair legs together while glued joints are drying. Loop the inner tube around the legs, and use a strip of wood to twist the rubber until it is stretched tight. Tie the strip to the inner tube to keep it from unwinding.

C-clamp Extender

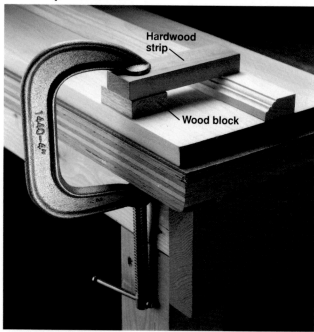

Hardwood strip

Wood block

When gluing wood trim to a flat workpiece, you can extend the reach of a C-clamp by using a short strip of scrap hardwood, and a small wood block that is the same thickness as the wood trim. Place the block close to the workpiece edge, then position the strip so it bridges the space between the block and the wood trim. Apply pressure to the strip with a C-clamp to hold the wood trim in place.

Gentle Jaws

Use a clothespin with the spring removed to clamp small, cylindrical items, like wooden dowels or plumbing tubes, in a bench vise. Small objects are hard to hold and can be damaged easily if clamped against the bare jaws of a vise.

Jumper Jaws

The alligator jaws from an old set of battery jumper cables make good general-purpose spring clamps. For example, use jaw clamps to hold small objects for spray painting. If needed, you can line the jaws with scraps of rubber inner tube to prevent damage to workpieces.

Cord Clamps

Keep electrical extension cords out of the way by clamping them in clothespins. Attach the clothespins to workshop walls and ceiling with screws or hot glue.

Spring-loaded Pliers

Turn an ordinary pliers into a spring clamp by tying a strip of rubber cut from an inner tube around the handles. Pad the jaws of the pliers with scraps of inner tube to prevent scratching a workpiece.

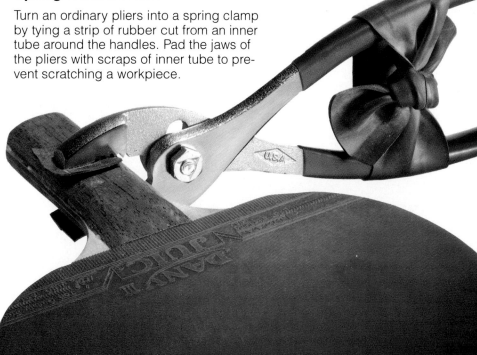

Tourniquet Clamp

Make a quick tourniquet clamp by tying a rope or nylon stocking around a workpiece. Use a screwdriver or stick to twist the rope until the loop tightens. Pad sharp workpiece corners with cardboard or rubber to protect the corners and prevent the rope from being cut. Tie the screwdriver to keep the rope from unwinding.

Long-distance Clamping

Use pairs of C-clamps to make extra-large clamps for holding frames while the glue dries. Tie a short piece of rope in a loop, then hook the stationary jaws of the C-clamps around the rope. Tighten the C-clamps to secure the workpiece.

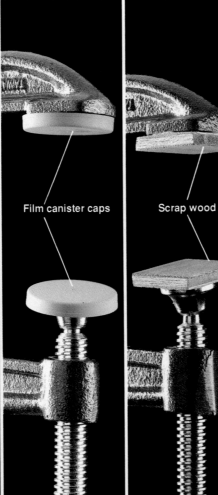

Felt

Film canister caps

Scrap wood

Protective Pads for Clamp Jaws

Protect workpiece surfaces when using C-clamps by padding the metal jaws. Use a hot glue gun to attach protective pads made from felt, plastic caps from film canisters, or small scraps of wood.

Pad Your Pliers

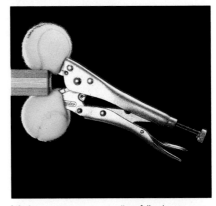

Make a temporary "soft" clamp from a pair of locking pliers. Cut slits in two old tennis balls and slide them over the plier jaws. The cloth-covered rubber protects workpiece surfaces.

Woodworker's Bench Vise

Line the jaws of a bench vise with wooden pads to prevent damage to workpieces. Each vise pad is made from two pieces of scrap plywood, and is oversized to provide better clamping. Use a jig saw to cut the frame (A) to match the shape of the vise jaws. Attach the frame to the pad faces (B) with carpenter's glue and brads.

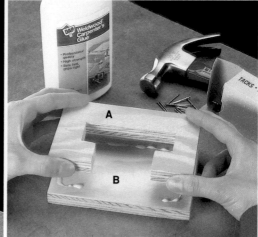

Iron-clad Clamping

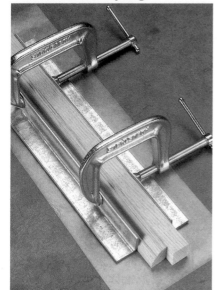

Distribute pressure and prevent bowing when clamping small pieces of wood by using two sections of angle iron and a pair of C-clamps. Angle irons also prevent clamps from damaging the wood.

True Grit for a Tight Grip

Get a better grip on smooth objects, like metal pipes, by gluing emery boards to the faces of vise jaws. The emery boards can be removed easily with a chisel or paint scraper when they are no longer needed.

Paired Pipe Clamps

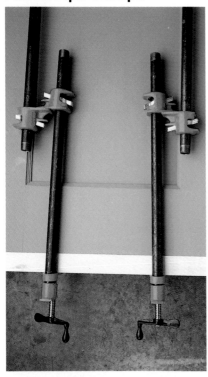

Double up two pipe clamps to grip a long workpiece. Position the clamps so the top jaws overlap, then tighten the clamps to secure the workpiece.

Highly Irregular

Irregularly shaped, delicate workpieces are difficult to grip with clamps. To hold pieces in place while glue dries, fill a plastic bag with sand and drape it over the workpiece. Sandbags of different sizes make handy hold-down aids in the workshop.

On a Pedestal

Pipe clamps and bar clamps are awkward to use when laid on a workbench. Mounting the clamps on 2 × 4 pedestals makes it easier to operate the clamp handles and provides better stability for a workpiece. Cut slots in the 2 × 4s to help keep the clamps aligned.

Clamp Power Tools in Place for Stationary Work

Hand power tools, like drills and sanders, can be anchored temporarily to a workbench with handscrew clamps. This technique is good for sanding small workpieces. Clamp the tool securely so it does not move, but do not damage the tool by overtightening the handscrew. A pad of soft foam or rubber under the handscrew jaw will help grip the tool while preventing damage to the tool casing.

C-clamp Miter Mate

Film cap

For accurate mitering of decorative moldings, the wood must be clamped securely in the miter saw. However, ordinary clamps can damage the contours of wood moldings. Make a simple miter clamp using a C-clamp, an old tennis ball, and a plastic cap from a film canister. Cut a small slice from the side cf the tennis ball, then hot-glue the film cap to the side opposite the slice, as shown above. When the miter clamp is attached to the miter saw, the soft rubber tennis ball holds the workpiece tightly without damaging the wood, and the plastic film cap keeps the C-clamp pad from slipping.

Upright Support

When painting or cutting plywood or paneling, you can support the sheet in an upright position by attaching a pair of pipe clamps to one edge, with the pipes facing in opposite directions. This technique also can be used to hold a door when drilling for locks, chiseling mortises, or planing an edge.

Rope Wrap

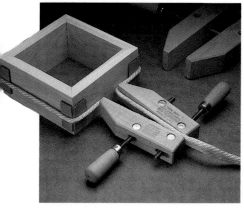

Make a quick rope clamp with a length of ½" nylon rope and a handscrew clamp. To use the clamp, close the back end of the handscrew around the ends of the rope. Wrap the rope around the workpiece, then tighten both clamp handles at the same time until the rope is taut.

Handy Handle

Keep a pipe clamp handy by using it as the handle for your wooden toolbox. The pipe clamp can be removed whenever you need to use it.

Door Support

These simple door clamps made from scrap lumber provide an easy way to hold doors in an upright position while installing locksets or hinges, or when planing an edge. The weight of the door causes the clamp to bend slightly and grip the sides of the door.

Each clamp requires two 2 × 4 uprights (A), 8" long; a ½" plywood cross member (B), 1½" × 16"; and two 2 × 4 foot pieces (C), 2½" long.

Join the pieces with carpenter's glue and wallboard screws. Space the uprights so the gap between them is equal to the thickness of the door. This design can be adapted to build clamps for holding framed storm windows or screens, plywood, and other sheet goods.

Vise-mounted Pipe Clamp

Decorative spindles and other long, slender workpieces can be end-clamped for sanding and finishing, using a pipe clamp secured inside a bench vise. To prevent the pipe clamp from slipping in the metal vise jaws, make a pipe holder from a pair of short, scrap 2 × 4s.

To make the pipe holder, clamp the 2 × 4s in the bench vise, then drill a hole along the seam between the boards. You may need a bit extender to make this hole. The diameter of the hole should be slightly less than the outside diameter of the pipe clamp.

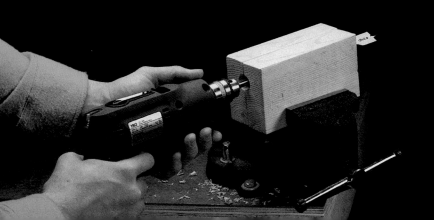

Band Together

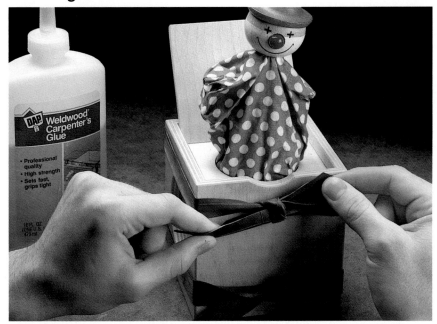

Make simple, inexpensive band clamps by cutting rubber strips from inner tubes. Wrap the strips around the workpiece and knot the ends. For greater holding power, increase the number of bands tied around the workpiece. Band clamps made from rubber will not damage workpiece surfaces or stick to wood glue.

Rope Tricks

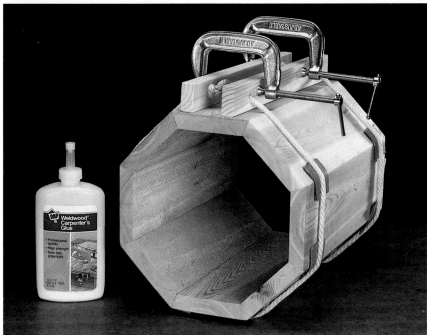

Clamp cylindrical workpieces with a double rope clamp made from a pair of 1 × 2s and two pieces of ½" nylon rope. Drill ⅝" holes near the ends of each 1 × 2, then thread the ropes through the holes and knot them. Place the double rope clamp around the workpiece, and tighten it by using C-clamps or handscrews to pull the 1 × 2s together.

Pipe-clamp Extender

If you do not have enough long pipe clamps, you can make pipe clamp extenders from scrap strips of ¾" plywood and short 2 × 4s.

Add a D-shaped cutout to the end of each plywood strip, then attach a 2 × 4 cleat to the opposite end, as shown above.

To use the extender, hook the 2 × 4 cleat over one end of the workpiece. Position the pipe clamp with the end jaw inside the cutout, and the handle jaw over the opposite end of the workpiece. Tighten the clamp to secure the workpiece.

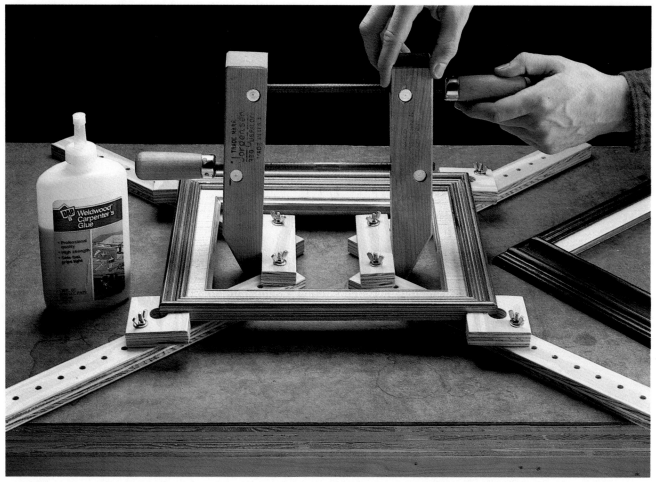

This easy-to-build miter clamp and one handscrew are all you need to make perfect frames.

Build a Four-corner Miter Clamp for Easy Frame-making

This adjustable miter clamp lets you clamp four corners at the same time when building picture frames or cabinet front frames. The miter clamp is built from scrap pieces of ¾" plywood, and is tightened with a single handscrew or bar clamp. The miter clamp adjusts to fit a variety of frame sizes.

For very large or very small frames, build additional miter clamps scaled to fit the frames.

Everything You Need:

Tools: pencil, framing square, jig saw, drill, bits (¼" twist, ¾" spade), handscrew or bar clamp.

Materials: scrap ¾" plywood, eight ¼" × 2" machine screws with washers and wing nuts.

Lumber Cutting List

Key	Pieces	Size and description
A	4	¾" clamp arms, 1½" × 16"
B	2	¾" cross bars, 1½" × 5"
C	4	¾" corner blocks, 2½" square

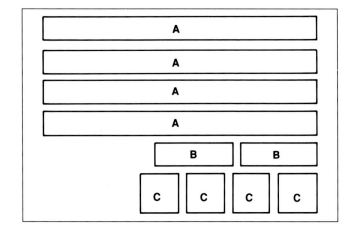

How to Build a Four-corner Miter Clamp

1 Draw a line lengthwise down the center of each miter clamp arm (A), using a framing square as a guide.

2 Mark locations for drill holes every 1" along the centerline on each arm. Drill a hole through the arm at each mark, using a ¼" bit.

3 Draw a line lengthwise down the center of each cross bar (B). Mark two points on each centerline, ¾" from the ends of the cross bar. Drill holes at each marked point, using a ¼" bit.

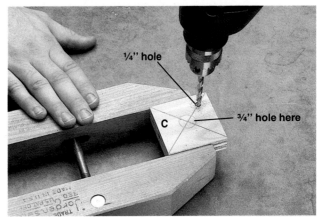

4 Draw a pair of diagonal lines across each corner block (C). On each block, mark a pivot point on one of the diagonal lines, ¾" from one corner. Drill a hole at the pivot point, using a ¼" bit. Drill another hole where diagonal lines intersect, using a ¾" bit.

5 Find the midpoint of each side of the corner block, and use these points to mark perpendicular lines across the block. Using the lines as a guide, cut away the corner that is opposite from the pivot point.

6 Assemble the four-corner miter clamp by loosely joining the parts with machine screws, washers, and wing nuts. Use the miter clamp as shown on the opposite page.

Instant Work Surface

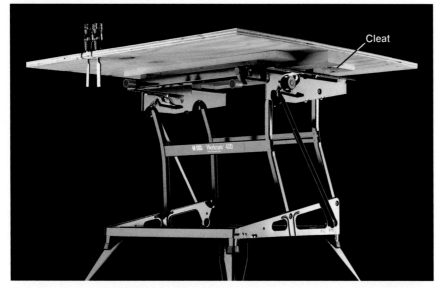

A clamping workbench, like the Workmate® work center, is convenient, portable, and easy to store. You can expand the working surface of a portable workbench by attaching a 4 ft. × 4 ft. piece of plywood to a 2 × 4 cleat. Lay the plywood on the work center, and clamp the cleat between the workbench jaws. Drill holes along the edge of the work surface to hold screwdrivers, chisels, and other small tools.

Versatile Accessory Clamps

Make clamping more convenient by using portable workbench accessories, such as bench stops (A), horizontal clamps (B), and hold-down clamps (C). To use these accessories with a standard workbench, drill mounting holes in the workbench top.

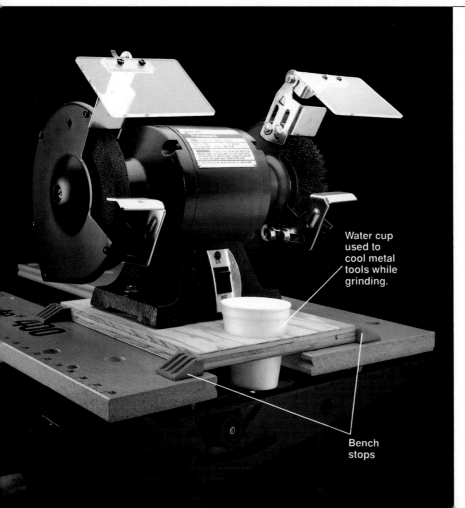

Water cup used to cool metal tools while grinding.

Bench stops

Put Bench Tools on a Pedestal

Mount small bench tools, like a bench grinder, band saw, or router table, on a portable workbench for safe and easy use. Attach the tool to a ¾" plywood pedestal, then place the tool on the workbench and clamp the pedestal between bench stops.

Grip in Groove

Clamp cylindrical workpieces, like metal pipes, between the jaws of the portable workbench. The edges of the jaws are grooved to help hold cylindrical objects more securely.

Easy Door Clamp

To clamp a door on edge when planing an edge or routing hinge mortises, position the door next to a portable workbench and clamp the end of the door in the workbench jaws.

Refurbish Your Portable Workbench

Refurbish a portable workbench by replacing the damaged surface material with a new top cut from 3/4" high-density particleboard or solid-core plywood. Use the old top as a template for making cutouts in the new workbench top, and reuse the old hardware. Use a router to cut grooves on the inside edge of each top piece for holding cylindrical objects.

Short Story

Make a "shorty" work station by retracting the lower legs on the workbench. Retracting the legs brings large workpieces down to a comfortable working height.

Clamp Down on It

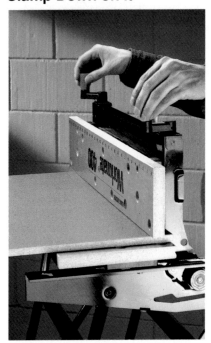

Large, flat workpieces can be clamped by rotating the movable jaw to a vertical position. Clamping in this position works well when routing edges on a workpiece.

Adhesive Type	Characteristics	Uses
White glue	**Strength:** moderate; rigid bond **Drying time:** several hours **Resistance to heat:** poor **Resistance to moisture:** poor **Hazards:** none **Cleanup/solvent:** soap and water	**Porous surfaces:** Wood (indoors) Paper Cloth
Yellow carpenter's glue	**Strength:** moderate to good; rigid bond **Drying time:** several hours; faster than white glue **Resistance to heat:** moderate **Resistance to moisture:** moderate **Hazards:** none **Cleanup/solvent:** soap and water	**Porous surfaces:** Wood (indoors) Paper Cloth
Two-part epoxy	**Strength:** excellent; strongest of all adhesives **Drying time:** varies, depending on manufacturer **Resistance to heat:** excellent **Resistance to moisture:** excellent **Hazards:** fumes are toxic and flammable **Cleanup/solvent:** acetone will dissolve some types	**Smooth & porous surfaces:** Wood (indoors & outdoors) Metal Masonry Glass Fiberglass
Hot glue	**Strength:** depends on type **Drying time:** less than 60 seconds **Resistance to heat:** fair **Resistance to moisture:** good **Hazards:** hot glue can cause burns **Cleanup/solvent:** heat will loosen bond	**Smooth & porous surfaces:** Glass Plastics Wood
Cyanoacrylate (instant) glue	**Strength:** excellent, but with little flexibility **Drying time:** a few seconds **Resistance to heat:** excellent **Resistance to moisture:** excellent **Hazards:** can bond skin instantly; toxic, flammable **Cleanup/solvent:** acetone	**Smooth surfaces:** Glass Ceramics Plastics Metal
Latex acrylic panel adhesive	**Strength:** good to excellent; very durable **Drying time:** 24 hours **Resistance to heat:** good **Resistance to moisture:** excellent **Hazards:** may irritate skin and eyes **Cleanup/solvent:** soap and water (while still wet)	**Porous surfaces:** Framing lumber Plywood and paneling Wallboard Foam panels Masonry
Water-base contact cement	**Strength:** good **Drying time:** bonds instantly; dries fully in 30 minutes **Resistance to heat:** excellent **Resistance to moisture:** good **Hazards:** may irritate skin and eyes **Cleanup/solvent:** soap and water (while still wet)	**Porous surfaces:** Plastic laminates Plywood Flooring Cloth
Silicone sealant	**Strength:** fair to good; very flexible bond **Drying time:** 24 hours **Resistance to heat:** good **Resistance to moisture:** excellent **Hazards:** may irritate skin and eyes **Cleanup/solvent:** acetone	**Smooth & porous surfaces:** Wood Porcelain Fiberglass Plastics Glass

Easy Fix for Wood Splinters

To apply glue to a wood splinter without breaking it off, use a matchbook cover. Apply a small amount of yellow carpenter's glue to the matchbook cover, then slide it under the wood sliver to coat it with glue. Wipe away excess glue with a damp cloth, then cover the splinter with wax paper or a scrap of rubber. Hold the splinter in place overnight with a wood block and C-clamp.

Avoid Sticky Situations

Glue seeping from wood joints can bond to a pipe clamp or C-clamp. Prevent this by placing wax paper between the clamp and the workpiece.

Spread Yourself Thin

For strong wood joints, the surfaces need a thin, even coating of glue. Make your own glue applicator from a thin strip of wood, a craft stick, a clothespin with a short piece of rope, or an old toothbrush.

Stick with Safe Glues

If you have a choice between water-based (latex) adhesives and solvent-based adhesives, always choose the latex products. Latex adhesives are less toxic than solvent-based products, are not flammable, and do not emit harmful vapors. Adhesives now available in latex form include contact cements, panel adhesives, and sealants. Identify latex products by looking for the words "water cleanup" or "latex" printed on their labels.

Furniture Fix

Regluing a loose furniture joint is difficult if the joint is dirty or caked with old glue and varnish. Before regluing, wash the joint with warm vinegar to remove caked-on glue. Rinse with clear water, and let the wood dry completely before gluing with yellow carpenter's glue.

Glue Gauge

When using epoxy adhesive, it is difficult to tell when it is dry. At the same time you apply adhesive to a workpiece, make a glue gauge by applying a small amount of epoxy to a piece of scrap wood. When the epoxy sample is dry, so is the workpiece.

Ready-to-go Glue

Store glue bottles upside down so the glue is ready to pour whenever it is needed. Make a glue bottle holder by drilling holes in a scrap 1 × 4 and attaching it to a wall or a pegboard storage panel.

How to Reglue Loose Veneer

1 Use a putty knife to gently pry up the edge of the loose veneer. Carefully scrape away the old glue.

2 Apply a thin coat of yellow carpenter's glue to the surfaces, using a cotton swab or craft stick. Press the veneer in place, and wipe away any excess carpenter's glue with a damp cloth.

3 Cover the glued area with wax paper or a scrap of rubber, and clamp it with a block of wood and a C-clamp. Let the glue dry overnight.

Getting out of a Bind

If you have trouble taking wood joints apart to repair them, try using a chemical solvent. Mineral spirits dissolve some adhesives, but the fumes are toxic and flammable. Acetone is a powerful solvent that dissolves most adhesives, but its fumes are highly toxic and very flammable. **Use these products only in well-ventilated areas.**

Nontoxic Remover for Tile Adhesive

Chemical solvents for removing tile adhesives are messy, toxic, and flammable. Instead of using chemical solvents, you may be able to use a heat gun to soften adhesives. Apply heat carefully so that the adhesive is softened but not scorched. Use a wide-blade wallboard knife to scrape away the adhesive. If you suspect that your tiles or tile adhesive contain asbestos, contact an asbestos-removal professional to have the tiles removed.

Remove Dried Glue with a Chisel

Carpenter's glue is nearly invisible when it dries — until you stain the wood (inset). To prevent streaks, remove dried glue before you start finishing, using a sharp chisel that has the corners rounded off to prevent gouging the wood. Hold the chisel with the bevel side down when scraping away dried glue.

Glue Trowel

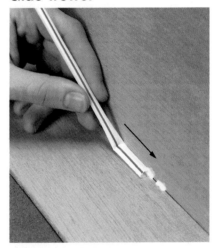

Remove excess glue from inside corners while it is still wet, using a drinking straw. Crease the straw near the tip and push it along the corner to remove the excess glue.

Less Mess

Cover your work surface with wax paper before setting a glued workpiece on it. The wax paper prevents seeping glue from bonding to the work surface.

Great Guns for Good Gluing

Use a hot glue gun instead of white household glue or yellow carpenter's glue to bond smooth surfaces, like plastic or glass. Most hot glues set up in less than 1 minute, so no clamping is required. The cordless hot glue gun shown above uses a small, replaceable butane fuel cartridge to heat the glue.

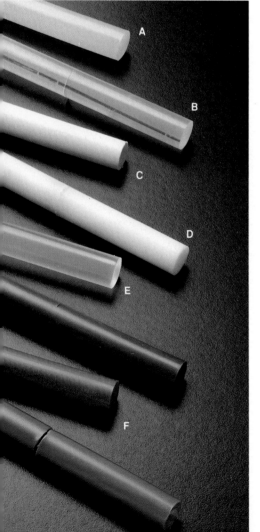

Walk Softly & Carry Several Sticks

Adhesive sticks for hot glue guns are available in several types for specialty uses.

(A) General-purpose adhesive dries clear, and is good for general bonding.

(B) Fast-drying adhesive, identified by a stripe, dries in 30 seconds or less.

(C) Wood-glue adhesive bonds well with wood fibers. It dries to an opaque cream color.

(D) Caulk/sealer adhesive is made to withstand changes in temperature and moisture, and can be used to weatherproof doors and windows.

(E) Ceramic/glass adhesive dries very quickly, and is invisible when dry.

(F) Craft adhesive comes in decorative colors to enhance your projects.

Nifty Nozzles

A needle nozzle is ideal for injecting glue into tight areas, and for small craft projects.

A wide spreader nozzle works well when gluing large surfaces or when filling large gaps with caulk-type adhesive.

Hot Caulker/Sealer

Fill small cracks around doors and windows using a hot glue gun loaded with caulk/sealer sticks. Hot glue guns work well in areas too small for a conventional glue gun, and in cool conditions where ordinary caulks become thick and difficult to apply.

Hot Glue Warm-up

Because hot glues dry very quickly, you may have trouble gluing large surfaces that require a lot of glue. Delay the drying time slightly by warming the workpiece surfaces with a heat gun before applying the adhesive. Apply the adhesive quickly, using a wide spreader nozzle (page opposite), and position the workpieces immediately.

Glue Gun Rack

Hot glue guns are useful tools, but they can be messy; and the hot metal tips can cause burns if the gun is not handled carefully.

The easy-to-make glue gun rack shown here works better than the built-in wire stands found on some glue guns. It provides a broad base to keep the hot glue gun from tipping over, and includes a drip-catcher.

The glue gun rack is built from a 4" × 8" wooden base (A), a 1" × 3" support block (B), a metal spring clip (C), and a metal jar lid (D). Join all the pieces together with hot glue.

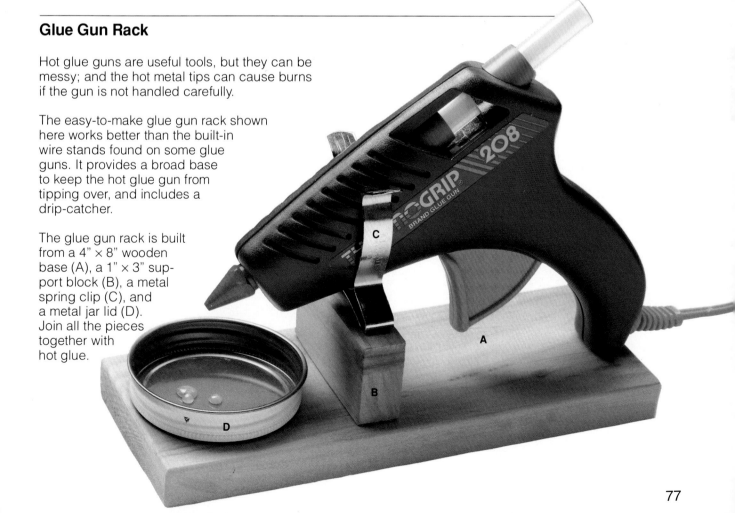

All in a Flap

Make your own flap sander for smoothing wood contours, using a 6" length of ⅜" wooden dowel and a 1" strip of cloth-backed sandpaper, such as that used for sanding belts. To make the flap sander, cut a 1" slot down the center of the dowel. Hot-glue the strip of cloth-backed sandpaper into the slot. Facing the slotted end of the dowel, wrap the sandpaper strip around the dowel in a clockwise direction. Attach the flap sander to a power drill.

Sanding Belt Cleaner

Extend the life of sanding belts by cleaning them with an old tennis shoe that has a natural rubber sole. Turn the sander on and press the tennis shoe against the belt for a few seconds. Wood dust trapped between the abrasives on the sanding belt will cling to the rubber sole of the shoe.

Sanding Extension

Make a sanding extension arm by taping sandpaper around the head of a sponge mop. The extension arm works well for sanding walls before painting, or for smoothing hard-to-reach wallboard joints.

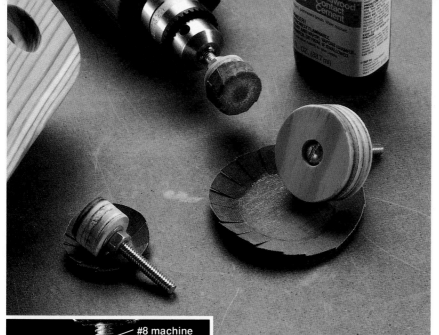

Hose It Down

Wrap a piece of sandpaper around a short length of old garden hose to make a sander for smoothing curves. If you wish, use hot glue to attach the sandpaper.

Disc-o Sander

Sand hard-to-reach recesses by making a custom-sized disc sander. Cut a small circle of finish plywood, and drill a countersunk hole through the center. Attach a machine screw to the plywood with a washer, lock washer, and nut. Attach the screw to the drill chuck. Cut a sandpaper disc and attach it the plywood circle with contact cement. To sand both the sides and bottom of a recess, cut the sandpaper disc larger than the plywood (above), then make slits in the edges and fold the sandpaper up around the plywood.

Image labels (Disc-o Sander cutaway):
#8 machine screw
Nut
Lock washer
¼" hole
Washer
½" counterbore
Contact cement
(Shown cut away)

Hold It Right There

When sanding a small, flat workpiece, hold it in place by laying it on a piece of carpet padding or sandpaper. To keep the padding or sandpaper from slipping, hot-glue it to the work surface.

In the Groove

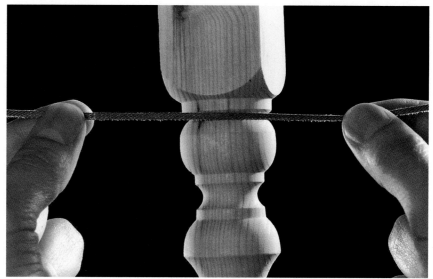

Sand hard-to-reach crevices in decorative spindles and millwork pieces with narrow strips cut from cloth-backed sanding belts.

Sandpaper Saw

Attach an old hacksaw blade to the edge of your workbench with screws, and use it as a convenient sandpaper cutter.

Stack the Deck

Wrap a piece of fine-grit sandpaper around an old deck of playing cards to make a contour sander that sands low points without flattening high points. The deck of cards shapes itself to the contours of the workpiece for quick and accurate sanding.

Just Your Size

Make a template to save time when cutting sandpaper sheets for a power sander. To make the template, cut a piece of ¾" lumber to match the sandpaper size your sander requires. Cut the edges of the template at a sharp-angled bevel to provide a cutting edge for tearing the paper.

Screen Sander

Wrap a piece of leftover window screening around a scrap 2 × 4 and staple it in place to make a good block sander for smoothing wallboard joints.

Plumbing: Tools, Materials & Skills

Tools for Plumbing

Many plumbing projects and repairs can be completed with basic hand tools you probably already own. Adding a few simple plumbing tools will prepare you for all the projects in this section. Specialty tools, such as a cast iron cutter or appliance dolly, are available at rental centers. When buying tools, invest in quality products.

Always care for tools properly. Clean tools after using them, wiping them free of dirt and dust with a soft rag. Prevent rust on metal tools by wiping them with a rag dipped in household oil. If a metal tool gets wet, dry it immediately, and then wipe it with an oiled rag. Keep tool boxes and cabinets organized. Make sure all tools are stored securely.

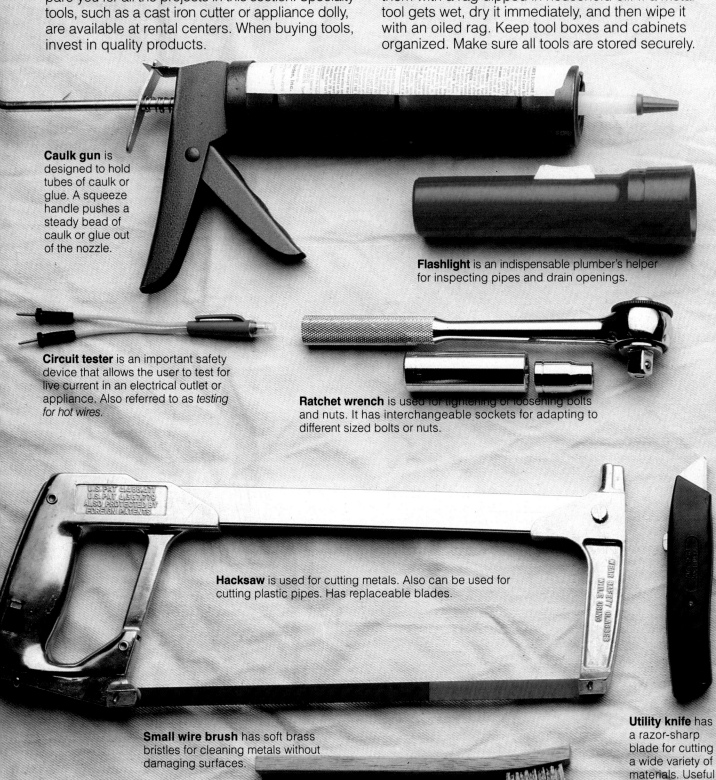

Caulk gun is designed to hold tubes of caulk or glue. A squeeze handle pushes a steady bead of caulk or glue out of the nozzle.

Flashlight is an indispensable plumber's helper for inspecting pipes and drain openings.

Circuit tester is an important safety device that allows the user to test for live current in an electrical outlet or appliance. Also referred to as *testing for hot wires*.

Ratchet wrench is used for tightening or loosening bolts and nuts. It has interchangeable sockets for adapting to different sized bolts or nuts.

Hacksaw is used for cutting metals. Also can be used for cutting plastic pipes. Has replaceable blades.

Small wire brush has soft brass bristles for cleaning metals without damaging surfaces.

Cold chisel is used with a *ball peen hammer* to cut or chip ceramic tile, mortar, or hardened metals.

Utility knife has a razor-sharp blade for cutting a wide variety of materials. Useful for trimming ends of plastic pipes. For safety, the utility knife should have a retractable blade.

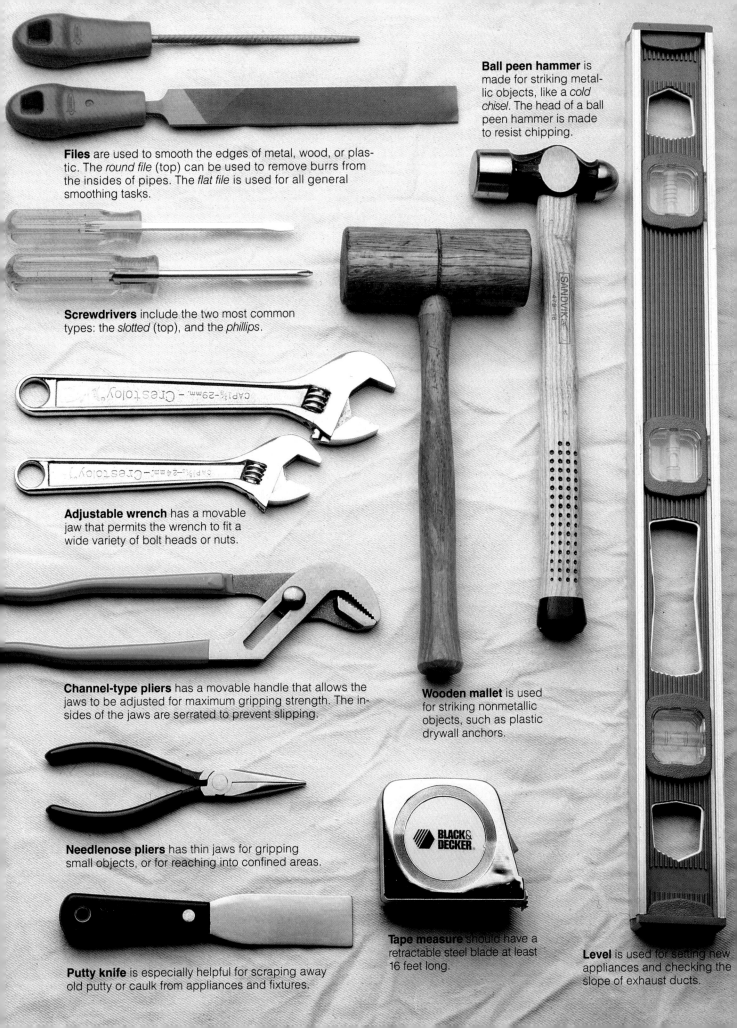

Files are used to smooth the edges of metal, wood, or plastic. The *round file* (top) can be used to remove burrs from the insides of pipes. The *flat file* is used for all general smoothing tasks.

Screwdrivers include the two most common types: the *slotted* (top), and the *phillips*.

Adjustable wrench has a movable jaw that permits the wrench to fit a wide variety of bolt heads or nuts.

Channel-type pliers has a movable handle that allows the jaws to be adjusted for maximum gripping strength. The insides of the jaws are serrated to prevent slipping.

Needlenose pliers has thin jaws for gripping small objects, or for reaching into confined areas.

Putty knife is especially helpful for scraping away old putty or caulk from appliances and fixtures.

Ball peen hammer is made for striking metallic objects, like a *cold chisel*. The head of a ball peen hammer is made to resist chipping.

Wooden mallet is used for striking nonmetallic objects, such as plastic drywall anchors.

Tape measure should have a retractable steel blade at least 16 feet long.

Level is used for setting new appliances and checking the slope of exhaust ducts.

Tubing cutter makes straight, smooth cuts in plastic and copper pipe. A tubing cutter usually has a dull, triangular blade, called a *reaming tip*, for removing burrs from the insides of pipes.

Closet auger is used to clear toilet clogs. It is a slender tube with a crank handle on one end of a flexible auger cable. A special bend in the tube allows the auger to be positioned in the bottom of the toilet bowl. The bend is usually protected with a rubber sleeve to prevent scratching the toilet.

Plastic tubing cutter works like a gardener's pruners to cut flexible plastic (PB) pipes quickly.

Spud wrench is specially designed for removing or tightening large nuts that are 2" to 4" in diameter. Hooks on the ends of the wrench grab onto the *lugs* of large nuts for increased leverage.

Plunger clears drain clogs with water and air pressure. The *flanged plunger* (shown) is used for toilet bowls. The flange usually can be folded up into the cup for use as a *standard plunger*. Use a standard plunger to clear clogs in sink, tub, shower, and floor drains.

Hand auger, sometimes called a *snake*, is used to clear clogs in drain lines. A long, flexible steel cable is stored in the disk-shaped crank. A pistol-grip handle allows the user to apply steady pressure on the cable.

Blow bag, sometimes called an *expansion nozzle*, is used to clear drains. It attaches to a garden hose and removes clogs with powerful spurts of water. The blow bag is best used on floor drains.

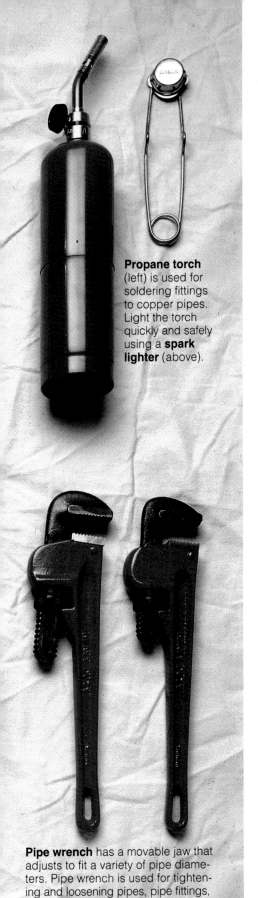

Propane torch (left) is used for soldering fittings to copper pipes. Light the torch quickly and safely using a **spark lighter** (above).

Pipe wrench has a movable jaw that adjusts to fit a variety of pipe diameters. Pipe wrench is used for tightening and loosening pipes, pipe fittings, and large nuts. Two pipe wrenches often are used together to prevent damage to pipes and fittings.

Power hand tools can make any job faster, easier, and safer. Cordless power tools offer added convenience. Use a cordless ⅜" **power drill** for virtually any drilling task. A cordless **power ratchet** makes it easy to turn small nuts or hex-head bolts. The cordless reversible **power screwdriver** drives a wide variety of screws and fasteners. A **reciprocating saw** uses interchangeable blades to cut wood, metal, or plastic. Thaw frozen pipes fast with a **heat gun.**

Rental tools may be needed for large jobs and special situations. A **power miter box** makes fast, accurate cuts in a wide variety of materials, including plastic pipes. A **motorized drain auger** clears tree roots from sewer service lines. Use an **appliance dolly** to move heavy objects like water heaters. A **cast iron cutter** is designed to cut tough cast-iron pipes. The **right-angle drill** is useful for drilling holes in hard-to-reach areas.

Plumbing Materials

Check local plumbing code for materials allowed in your area. All diameters specified are the interior diameters (I.D.) of pipes.

Benefits & Characteristics

Cast iron is very strong, but is difficult to cut and fit. Repairs and replacements should be made with plastic pipe, if allowed by local code.

ABS (Acrylonitrile-Butadiene-Styrene) was the first rigid plastic approved for use in home drain systems. Some local plumbing codes now restrict the use of ABS in new installations.

PVC (Poly-Vinyl-Chloride) is a modern rigid plastic that is highly resistant to damage by heat or chemicals. It is the best material for drain-waste-vent pipes.

Galvanized iron is very strong, but gradually will corrode. Not advised for new installation. Because galvanized iron is difficult to cut and fit, large jobs are best left to a professional.

CPVC (Chlorinated-Poly-Vinyl-Chloride) rigid plastic is chemically formulated to withstand the high temperatures and pressures of water supply systems. Pipes and fittings are inexpensive.

PB (Poly-Butylene) flexible plastic is easy to fit. It bends easily around corners and requires fewer fittings than CPVC. Not all local codes have been updated to permit use of PB pipe.

Rigid copper is the best material for water supply pipes. It resists corrosion, and has smooth surfaces that provide good water flow. Soldered copper joints are very durable.

Chromed copper has an attractive shiny surface, and is used in areas where appearance is important. Chromed copper is durable and easy to bend and fit.

Flexible copper tubing is easy to shape, and will withstand a slight frost without rupturing. Flexible copper bends easily around corners, so it requires fewer fittings than rigid copper.

Brass is heavy and durable. **Chromed brass** has an attractive shiny surface, and is used for drain traps where appearance is important.

Common Uses	Lengths	Diameters	Fitting Methods	Tools Used for Cutting
Main drain-waste-vent pipes	5 ft., 10 ft.	3", 4"	Joined with banded neoprene couplings	Cast iron cutter or hacksaw
Drain & vent pipes; drain traps	10 ft., 20 ft.; or sold by linear ft.	1½", 2", 3", 4"	Joined with solvent glue and plastic fittings	Tubing cutter, miter box, or hacksaw
Drain & vent pipes; drain traps	10 ft., 20 ft.; or sold by linear ft.	1½", 2", 3", 4"	Joined with solvent glue and plastic fittings	Tubing cutter, miter box, or hacksaw
Drains; hot & cold water supply pipes	1" to 1-ft. nipples; custom lengths up to 20 ft.	½", ¾", 1", 1½", 2"	Joined with galvanized threaded fittings	Hacksaw or reciprocating saw
Hot & cold water supply pipes	10 ft.	⅜", ½", ¾", 1"	Joined with solvent glue and plastic fittings, or with grip fittings	Tubing cutter, miter box, or hacksaw
Hot & cold water supply, where allowed by code	25-ft., 100-ft. coils; or sold by linear ft.	⅜", ½", ¾"	Joined with plastic grip fittings	Flexible plastic tubing cutter, sharp knife, or miter box
Hot & cold water supply pipes	10 ft., 20 ft.; or sold by linear ft.	⅜", ½", ¾", 1"	Joined with metal solder or compression fittings	Tubing cutter, hacksaw, or jig saw
Supply tubing for plumbing fixtures	12", 20", 30"	⅜"	Joined with brass compression fittings	Tubing cutter or hacksaw
Gas tubing; hot & cold water supply tubing	30-ft., 60-ft. coils; or sold by linear ft.	¼", ⅜", ½", ¾", 1"	Joined with brass flare fittings, compression fittings, or metal solder	Tubing cutter or hacksaw
Valves & shutoffs; chromed drain traps	Lengths vary	¼", ½", ¾"; *for drain traps:* 1¼", 1½"	Joined with compression fittings, or with metal solder	Tubing cutter, hacksaw, or reciprocating saw

Water Supply Fittings

Copper   Galvanized   CPVC
          iron

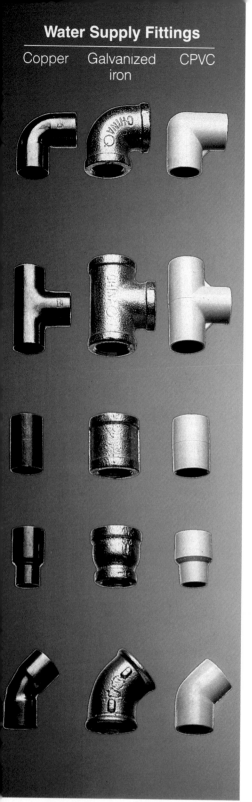

Drain-Waste-Vent Fittings

ABS   PVC

90° elbows are used to make right-angle bends in a pipe run. Drain-waste-vent (DWV) elbows are curved to prevent debris from being trapped in the bend.

T-fittings are used to connect branch lines in water supply and drain-waste-vent systems. A T-fitting used in a DWV system is called a "waste-T" or "sanitary T."

Couplings are used to join two straight pipes. Special transition fittings (page opposite) are used to join two pipes that are made from different materials.

Reducers connect pipes of different diameters. Reducing T-fittings and elbows are also available.

45° elbows are used to make gradual bends in a pipe run. Elbows are also available with 60° and 72° bends.

Plumbing Fittings

Plumbing fittings come in different shapes to let you form branch lines, change the direction of a pipe run, or connect pipes of different sizes. Transition fittings are used to connect pipes and fixtures that are made from different materials (page opposite). Fittings come in many sizes, but the basic shapes are standard to all metal and plastic pipes. In general, fittings used to connect drain pipes have gradual bends for a smooth flow of drain water.

How to Use Transition Fittings

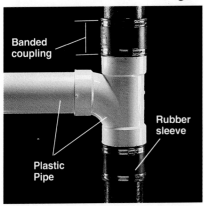

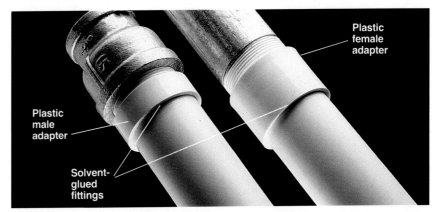

Connect plastic to cast iron with banded couplings (pages 114 to 117). Rubber sleeves cover ends of pipes and ensure a watertight joint.

Connect plastic to threaded metal pipes with male and female threaded adapters. Plastic adapter is solvent-glued to plastic pipe. Threads of pipe should be wrapped with Teflon™ tape. Metal pipe is then screwed directly to the adapter.

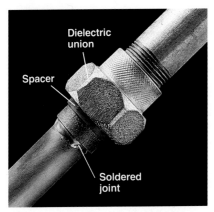

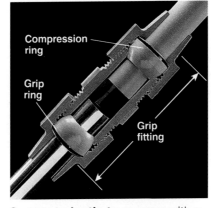

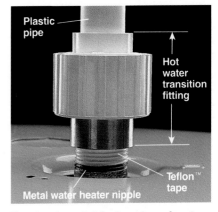

Connect copper to galvanized iron with a dielectric union. Union is threaded onto iron pipe, and is soldered to copper pipe. A dielectric union has plastic spacer that prevents corrosion caused by electrochemical reaction between metals.

Connect plastic to copper with a grip fitting. Each side of the fitting (shown in cutaway) contains a narrow grip ring and a plastic compression ring (or rubber O-ring) that forms the seal.

Connect metal hot water pipe to plastic with a hot water transition fitting that prevents leaks caused by different expansion rates of materials. Metal pipe threads are wrapped with Teflon™ tape. Plastic pipe is solvent-glued to fitting.

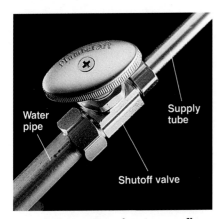

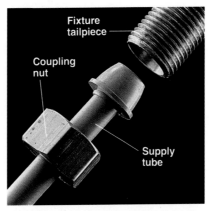

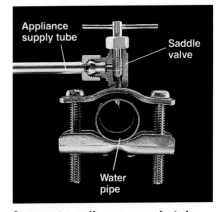

Connect a water pipe to any fixture supply tube, using a shutoff valve.

Connect any supply tube to a fixture tailpiece with a coupling nut. Coupling nut seals the bell-shaped end of supply tube against the fixture tailpiece.

Connect appliance supply tube to copper pipe with a saddle valve. Saddle valve (shown in cutaway) often is used to connect a refrigerator icemaker.

Working with Copper

Copper is the ideal material for water supply pipes. It resists corrosion and has smooth surfaces that provide good water flow. Copper pipes are available in several diameters (page 87) but most home water supply systems use ½" or ¾" pipe. Copper pipe is manufactured in rigid and flexible forms.

Rigid copper, sometime called hard copper, is approved for home water supply systems by all local codes. It comes in three wall-thickness grades: Types M, L, and K. Type M is the thinnest, the least expensive, and a good choice for do-it-yourself home plumbing.

Rigid Type L usually is required by codes for commercial plumbing systems. Because it is strong and solders easily, Type L may be preferred by some professional plumbers and do-it-yourselfers for home use. Type K has the heaviest wall thickness, and is used most often for underground water service lines.

Flexible copper, also called soft copper, comes in two wall-thickness grades: Types L and K. Both are approved for most home water supply systems, although flexible Type L copper is used primarily for gas service lines. Because it is bendable and will resist a mild frost, Type L may be installed as part of a water supply system in unheated indoor areas, like crawl spaces. Type K is used for underground water service lines.

A third form of copper, called DWV, is used for drain systems. Because most codes now allow low-cost plastic pipes for drain systems, DWV copper is seldom used.

Copper pipes are connected with soldered, compression, or flare fittings (see chart below). Always follow your local code for the correct types of pipes and fittings allowed in your area.

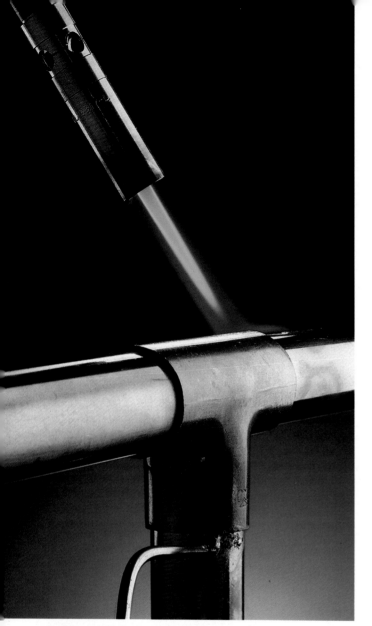

Soldered fittings, also called sweat fittings, often are used to join copper pipes. Correctly soldered fittings (pages 92 to 96) are strong and trouble-free. Copper pipe can also be joined with compression fittings (pages 98 to 99) or flare fittings (pages 100 to 101). See chart below.

Copper Pipe & Fitting Chart

Fitting Method	Rigid Copper			Flexible Copper		General Comments
	Type M	Type L	Type K	Type L	Type K	
Soldered	yes	yes	yes	yes	yes	Inexpensive, strong, and trouble-free fitting method. Requires some skill.
Compression	yes	not recommended		yes	yes	Easy to use. Allows pipes or fixtures to be repaired or replaced readily. More expensive than solder. Best used on flexible copper.
Flare	no	no	no	yes	yes	Use only with flexible copper pipes. Usually used as a gas-line fitting. Requires some skill.

90

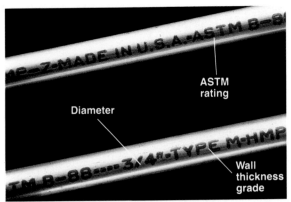

Grade stamp information includes pipe diameter, the wall-thickness grade, and a stamp of approval from the ASTM (American Society for Testing and Materials). Type M pipe is identified by red lettering, Type L by blue lettering.

Bend flexible copper pipe with a coil-spring tubing bender to avoid kinks. Select a bender that matches the outside diameter of the pipe. Slip bender over pipe using a twisting motion. Bend pipe slowly until it reaches the correct angle, but not more than 90°.

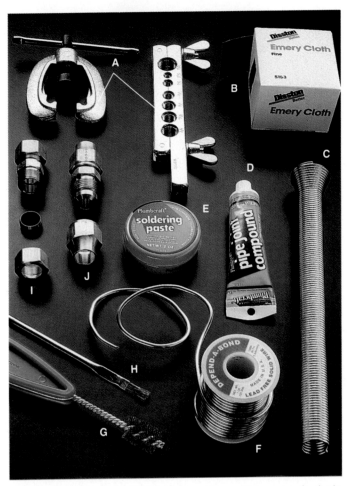

Specialty tools & materials for working with copper include: flaring tool (A), emery cloth (B), coil-spring tubing bender (C), pipe joint compound (D), self-cleaning soldering paste (flux) (E), lead-free solder (F), wire brush (G), flux brush (H), compression fitting (I), flare fitting (J).

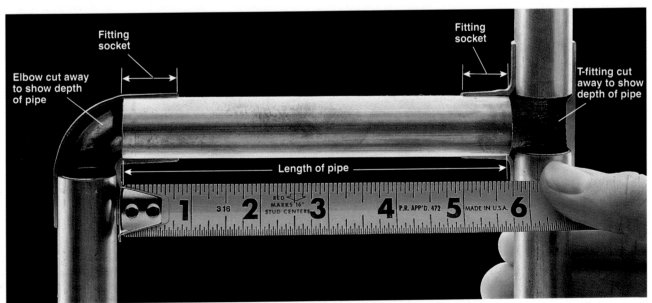

Find length of copper pipe needed by measuring between the bottom of the copper fitting sockets (fittings shown in cutaway). Mark length on the pipe with a felt-tipped pen.

91

Cutting & Soldering Copper

The best way to cut rigid and flexible copper pipe is with a tubing cutter. A tubing cutter makes a smooth, straight cut, an important first step toward making a watertight joint. Remove any metal burrs on the cut edges with a reaming tool or round file.

Copper can be cut with a hacksaw. A hacksaw is useful in tight areas where a tubing cutter will not fit. Take care to make a smooth, straight cut when cutting with a hacksaw.

A soldered pipe joint, also called a sweated joint, is made by heating a copper or brass fitting with a propane torch until the fitting is just hot enough to melt metal solder. The heat draws the solder into the gap between the fitting and pipe to form a watertight seal. A fitting that is overheated or unevenly heated will not draw in solder. Copper pipes and fittings must be clean and dry to form a watertight seal.

Protect wood from heat of the torch flame while soldering, using a double layer (two 18" × 18" pieces) of 26-gauge sheet metal. Buy sheet metal at hardware stores or building supply centers, and keep it to use with all soldering projects.

Everything You Need:

Tools: tubing cutter with reaming tip (or hacksaw and round file), wire brush, flux brush, propane torch, spark lighter (or matches), adjustable wrench, channel-type pliers.

Materials: copper pipe, copper fittings, emery cloth, soldering paste (flux), sheet metal, lead-free solder, rag.

Soldering Tips

Use caution when soldering copper. Pipes and fittings become very hot and must be allowed to cool before handling.

Keep joint dry when soldering existing water pipes by plugging the pipe with bread. Bread absorbs moisture that may ruin the soldering process and cause pinhole leaks. The bread dissolves when water is turned back on.

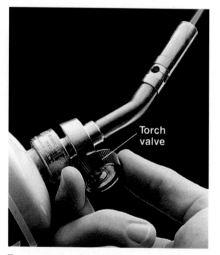

Torch valve

Prevent accidents by shutting off propane torch immediately after use. Make sure valve is closed completely.

How to Cut Rigid & Flexible Copper Pipe

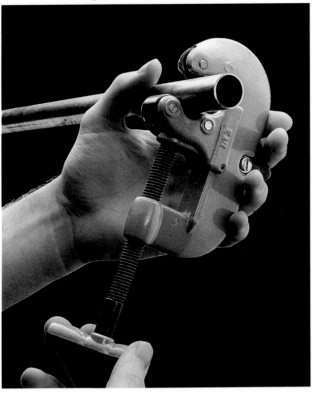

1 Place tubing cutter over the pipe and tighten the handle so that pipe rests on both rollers, and cutting wheel is on marked line.

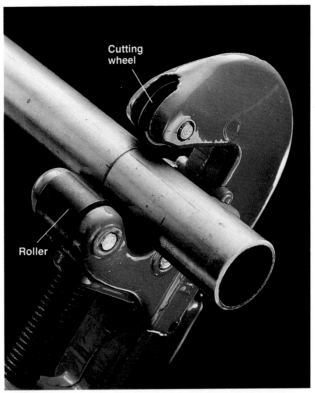

2 Turn tubing cutter one rotation so that cutting wheel scores a continuous straight line around the pipe.

3 Rotate the cutter in the opposite direction, tightening the handle slightly after every two rotations, until cut is complete.

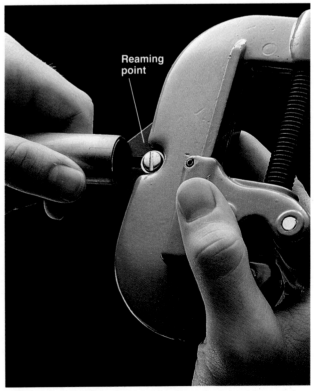

4 Remove sharp metal burrs from inside edge of the cut pipe, using the reaming point on the tubing cutter, or a round file.

How to Solder Copper Pipes & Fittings

1 Clean end of each pipe by sanding with emery cloth. Ends must be free of dirt and grease to ensure that the solder forms a good seal.

2 Clean inside of each fitting by scouring with a wire brush or emery cloth.

Flux brush

soldering paste

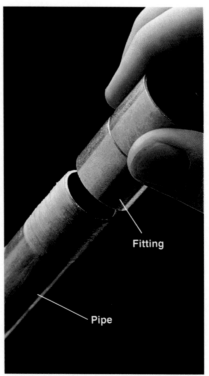

Fitting

Pipe

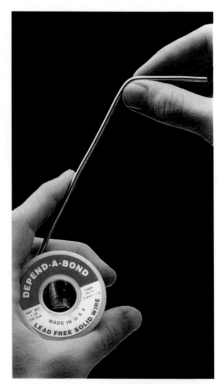

3 Apply a thin layer of soldering paste (flux) to end of each pipe, using a flux brush. Soldering paste should cover about 1" of pipe end.

4 Assemble each joint by inserting the pipe into fitting so it is tight against the bottom of the fitting sockets. Twist each fitting slightly to spread soldering paste.

5 Prepare the wire solder by unwinding 8" to 10" of wire from spool. Bend the first 2" of the wire to a 90° angle.

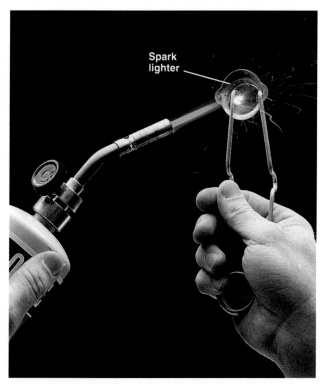

Spark
lighter

6 Light propane torch by opening valve and striking a spark lighter or a match next to the torch nozzle until the gas ignites.

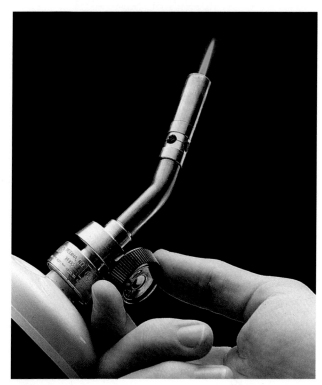

7 Adjust the torch valve until the inner portion of the flame is 1'' to 2'' long.

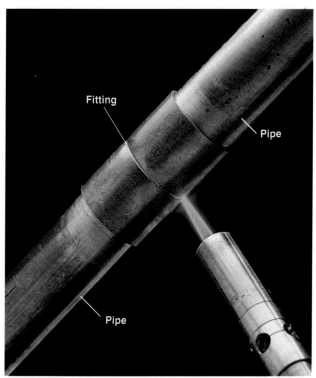

Fitting

Pipe

Pipe

8 Hold flame tip against middle of fitting for 4 to 5 seconds, until soldering paste begins to sizzle.

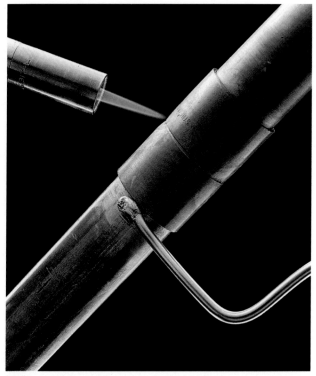

9 Heat other side of copper fitting to ensure that heat is distributed evenly. Touch solder to pipe. If solder melts, pipe is ready to be soldered.

(continued next page)

How to Solder Copper Pipes & Fittings (continued)

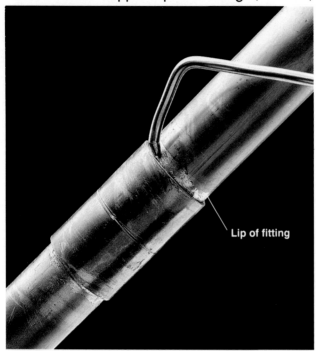

Lip of fitting

10 When pipe is hot enough to melt solder, remove torch and quickly push ½'' to ¾'' of solder into each joint. Capillary action fills joint with liquid solder. A correctly soldered joint should show a thin bead of solder around the lip of the fitting.

11 Wipe away excess solder with a dry rag. **Caution: pipes will be hot.** When all joints have cooled, turn on water and check for leaks. If joint leaks, drain pipes, apply additional soldering paste to rim of joint, and resolder.

How to Solder Brass Valves

1 Remove the valve stem with an adjustable wrench. Removing the stem prevents heat damage to rubber or plastic stem parts while soldering. Prepare the copper pipes (page 94) and assemble joints.

2 Light propane torch (page 95). Heat body of valve, moving flame to distribute heat evenly. Brass is denser than copper, so it requires more heating time before joints will draw solder. Apply solder (pages 94 to 96). Let metal cool, then reassemble valve.

How to Take Apart Soldered Joints

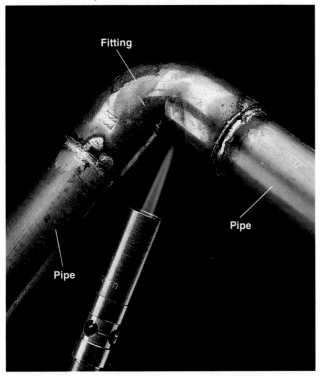

1 Turn off the water and drain the pipes by opening the highest and lowest faucets in the house. Light propane torch (page 95). Hold flame tip to the fitting until the solder becomes shiny and begins to melt.

2 Use channel-type pliers to separate the pipes from the fitting.

3 Remove old solder by heating ends of pipe with propane torch. Use dry rag to wipe away melted solder quickly. **Caution: pipes will be hot.**

4 Use emery cloth to polish ends of pipe down to bare metal. Never reuse old fittings.

Using Compression Fittings

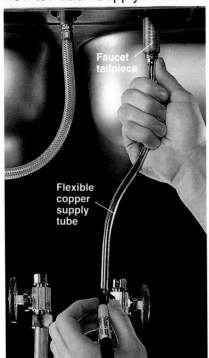

Compression fitting (shown in cutaway) shows how threaded compression nut forms seal by forcing the compression ring against the copper pipe. Compression ring is covered with pipe joint compound before assembling to ensure a perfect seal.

Compression fittings are used to make connections that may need to be taken apart. Compression fittings are easy to disconnect, and often are used to install supply tubes and fixture shutoff valves (sequence below). Use compression fittings in places where it is unsafe or difficult to solder, such as in a crawl space.

Compression fittings are used most often with flexible copper pipe. Flexible copper is soft enough to allow the compression ring to seat snugly, creating a watertight seal. Compression fittings also may be used to make connections with Type M rigid copper pipe. See the chart on page 90.

Everything You Need:

Tools: felt-tipped pen, tubing cutter or hacksaw, adjustable wrenches.

Materials: brass compression fittings, pipe joint compound.

How to Attach Supply Tubes to Fixture Shutoff Valves with Compression Fittings

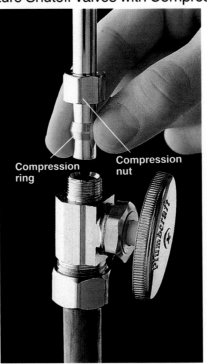

1 Bend flexible copper supply tube, and mark to length. Include ½" for portion that will fit inside valve. Cut tube (page 93).

2 Slide the compression nut and then the compression ring over end of pipe. Threads of nut should face the valve.

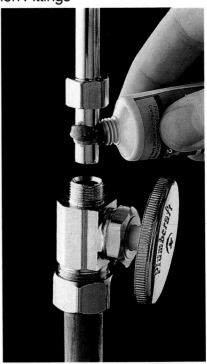

3 Apply a layer of pipe joint compound over the compression ring. Joint compound helps ensure a watertight seal.

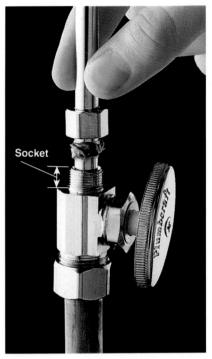

4 Insert end of pipe into fitting so it fits flush against bottom of fitting socket.

5 Slide compression ring and nut against threads of valve. Hand-tighten nut onto valve.

6 Tighten compression nut with adjustable wrenches. Do not overtighten. Turn on water and watch for leaks. If fitting leaks, tighten nut gently.

How to Join Two Copper Pipes with a Compression Union Fitting

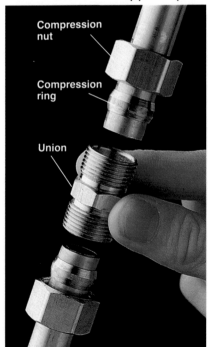

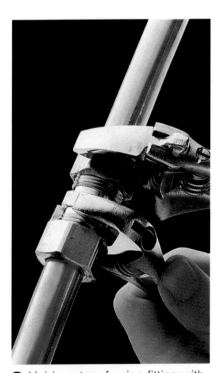

1 Slide compression nuts and rings over ends of pipes. Place threaded union between pipes.

2 Apply a layer of pipe joint compound to compression rings, then screw compression nuts onto threaded union.

3 Hold center of union fitting with an adjustable wrench, and use another wrench to tighten each compression nut one complete turn. Turn on water. If fitting leaks, tighten nuts gently.

Using Flare Fittings

Flare fittings are used most often for flexible copper gas lines. Flare fittings may be used with flexible copper water supply pipes, but they cannot be used where the connections will be concealed inside walls. Always check your local codes regarding the use of flare fittings.

Flare fittings are easy to disconnect. Use a flare fitting in places where it is unsafe or difficult to solder, such as in a crawl space.

Everything You Need:

Tools: two-piece flaring tool, adjustable wrenches.

Materials: brass flare fittings.

Flare fitting (shown in cutaway) shows how flared end of flexible copper pipe forms seal against the head of a brass union fitting.

Flare nut

Flared end of pipe

Brass union fitting

Flare nut

Flared end of pipe

Flexible copper pipe

How to Join Two Copper Pipes with a Flare Union Fitting

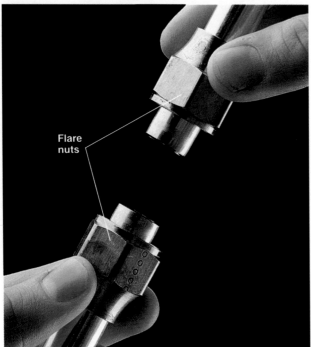

Flare nuts

1 Slide flare nuts onto ends of pipes. Nuts must be placed on pipes before ends can be flared.

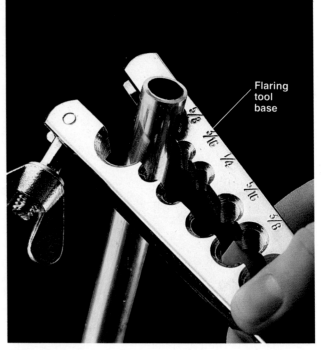

Flaring tool base

2 Select hole in flaring tool base that matches outside diameter of pipe. Open base, and place end of pipe inside hole.

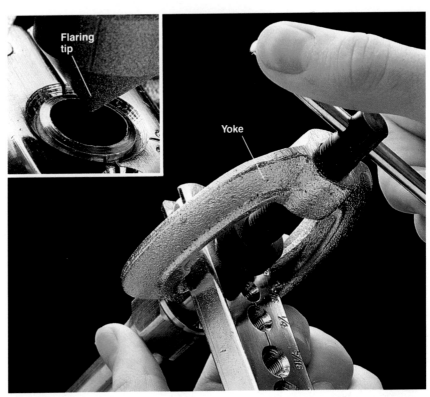

3 Clamp pipe inside flaring tool base. End of pipe must be flush with flat surface of base.

4 Slip yoke of flaring tool around base. Center flaring tip of yoke over end of pipe (inset photo above). Tighten handle of yoke to shape the end of the pipe. Flare is completed when handle cannot be turned further.

5 Remove yoke, and remove pipe from base. Repeat flaring for other pipe.

6 Place flare union between flared ends of pipe, and screw flare nuts onto union.

7 Hold center of flare union with adjustable wrench, and use another wrench to tighten flare nuts one complete turn. Turn on water. If fitting leaks, tighten nuts.

Working with Plastics

Plastic pipes and fittings are popular with do-it-yourselfers because they are lightweight, inexpensive, and easy to use. Local plumbing codes increasingly are approving the use of plastics for home plumbing.

Plastic pipes are available in rigid and flexible forms. Rigid plastics include ABS (Acrylonitrile-Butadiene-Styrene), PVC (Poly-Vinyl-Chloride), and CPVC (Chlorinated-Poly-Vinyl-Chloride). The most commonly used flexible plastic is PB (Poly-Butylene).

ABS and PVC are used in drain systems. PVC is a newer form of plastic that resists chemical damage and heat better than ABS. It is approved for above-ground use by all plumbing codes. However, some codes still require cast-iron pipe for main drains that run under concrete slabs.

CPVC and PB are used in water supply systems. Rigid CPVC pipe and fittings are less expensive than PB, but flexible PB pipe is a good choice in cramped locations, because it bends easily and requires fewer fittings.

Plastic pipes can be joined to existing iron or copper pipes using transition fittings (page 89), but different types of plastic should not be joined. For example, if your drain pipes are ABS plastic, use only ABS pipes and fittings when making repairs and replacements.

Prolonged exposure to sunlight eventually can weaken plastic plumbing pipe, so plastics should not be installed or stored in areas that receive constant direct sunlight.

Metal pipe

Metal pipe

Jumper wire

Ground clamp

Plastic pipe

Caution: Your home electrical system could be grounded through metal water pipes. When adding plastic pipes to a metal plumbing system, make sure the electrical ground circuit is not broken. Use ground clamps and jumper wires, available at any hardware store, to bypass the plastic transition and complete the electrical ground circuit. Clamps must be firmly attached to bare metal on both sides of the plastic pipe.

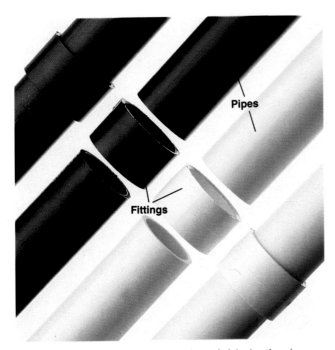

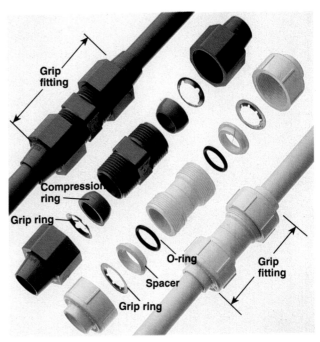

Solvent-glued fittings are used on rigid plastic pipes. Solvent dissolves a thin layer of plastic, and bonds the pipe and fitting together.

Grip fittings are used to join flexible PB pipes, and can also be used for CPVC pipes. Grip fittings come in two styles. One type (left) resembles a copper compression fitting. It has a metal grip ring and a plastic compression ring. The other type (right) has a rubber O-ring instead of a compression ring.

Plastic Pipe Grade Stamps

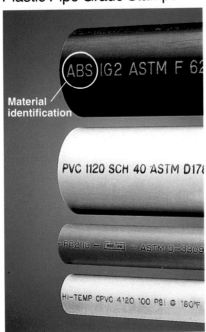

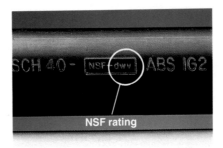

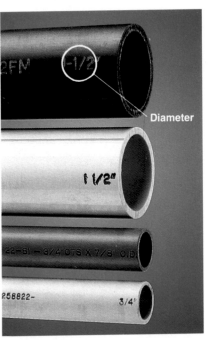

Material identification: For sink traps and drain pipes, use PVC or ABS pipe. For water supply pipes, use PB or CPVC pipe.

NSF rating: For sink traps and drains, choose PVC or ABS pipe that has a DWV (drain-waste-vent) rating from the National Sanitation Foundation (NSF). For water supply pipes, choose PB or CPVC pipe that has a PW (pressurized water) rating.

Pipe diameter: PVC and ABS pipes for drains usually have an inside diameter of 1¼" to 4". PB and CPVC pipes for water supply usually have an inside diameter of ½" or ¾".

Cutting & Fitting Plastic Pipe

Cut rigid ABS, PVC, or CPVC plastic pipes with a tubing cutter, or with any saw. Cuts must be straight to ensure watertight joints.

Rigid plastics are joined with plastic fittings and solvent glue. Use a solvent glue that is made for the type of plastic pipe you are installing. For example, do not use ABS solvent on PVC pipe. Some solvent glues, called "all-purpose" or "universal" solvents, may be used on all types of plastic pipe.

Solvent glue hardens in about 30 seconds, so test-fit all plastic pipes and fittings before gluing the first joint. For best results, the surfaces of plastic pipes and fittings should be dulled with emery cloth and liquid primer before they are joined.

Liquid solvent glues and primers are toxic and flammable. Provide adequate ventilation when fitting plastics, and store the products away from any source of heat.

Cut flexible PB pipes with a plastic tubing cutter, or with a knife. Make sure cut ends of pipe are straight. Join PB plastic pipes with plastic grip fittings. Grip fittings also are used to join rigid or flexible plastic pipes to copper plumbing pipes (page 89).

Specialty materials for plastics include: solvent glues and primer (A), solvent-glue fittings (B), emery cloth (C), plastic grip fittings (D), and petroleum jelly (E).

Everything You Need:

Tools: tape measure, felt-tipped pen, tubing cutter (or miter box or hacksaw), utility knife, channel-type pliers.

Materials: plastic pipe, fittings, emery cloth, plastic pipe primer, solvent glue, rag, petroleum jelly.

Measuring Plastic Pipe

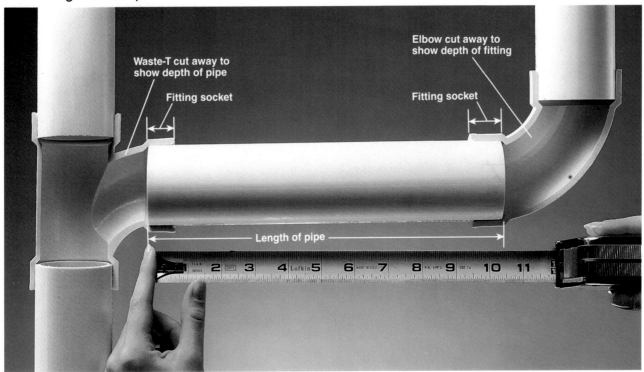

Find length of plastic pipe needed by measuring between the bottoms of the fitting sockets (fittings shown in cutaway). Mark the length on the pipe with a felt-tipped pen.

How to Cut Rigid Plastic Pipe

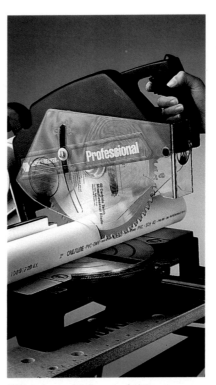

Tubing cutter: Tighten tool around pipe so cutting wheel is on marked line (page 93). Rotate tool around pipe, tightening screw every two rotations, until pipe snaps.

Miter box: Make straight cuts on all types of plastic pipe with a power or hand miter box.

Hacksaw: Clamp plastic pipe in a portable gripping bench or a vise, and keep the hacksaw blade straight while sawing.

How to Solvent-glue Rigid Plastic Pipe

1 Remove rough burrs on cut ends of plastic pipe, using a utility knife.

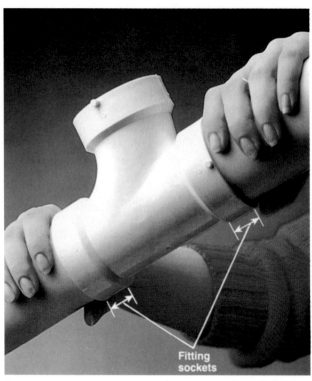

2 Test-fit all pipes and fittings. Pipes should fit tightly against the bottom of the fitting sockets.

Fitting sockets

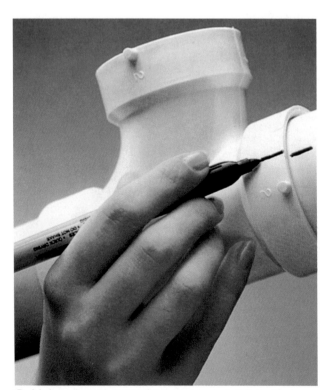

3 Make alignment marks across each joint with a felt-tipped pen.

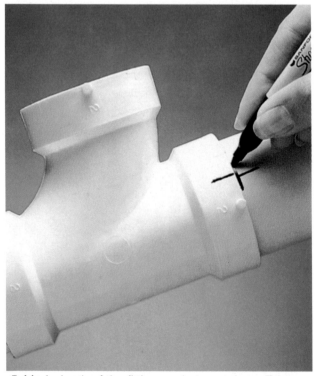

4 Mark depth of the fitting sockets on pipes. Take pipes apart.

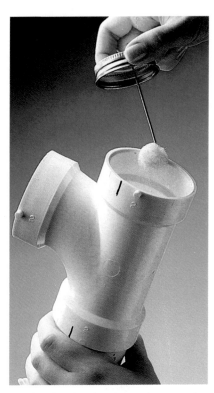

5 Clean ends of pipes and the fitting sockets with emery cloth.

6 Apply plastic pipe primer to the ends of the pipes. Primer dulls glossy surfaces and ensures a good seal.

7 Apply plastic pipe primer to the insides of the fitting sockets.

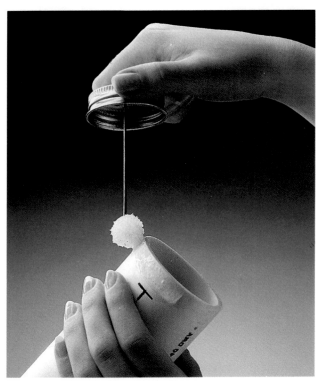

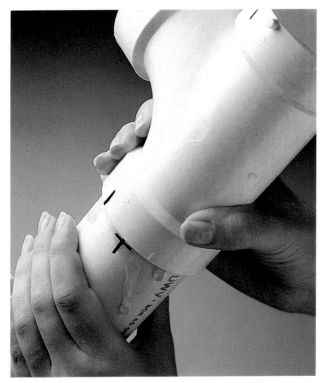

8 Solvent-glue each joint by applying a thick coat of solvent glue to end of pipe. Apply a thin coat of solvent glue to inside surface of fitting socket. Work quickly: solvent glue hardens in about 30 seconds.

9 Quickly position pipe and fitting so that alignment marks are offset by about 2 inches. Force pipe into fitting until the end fits flush against the bottom of the socket. Twist pipe into alignment (step 10).

(continued next page)

How to Solvent-glue Rigid Plastic Pipe (continued)

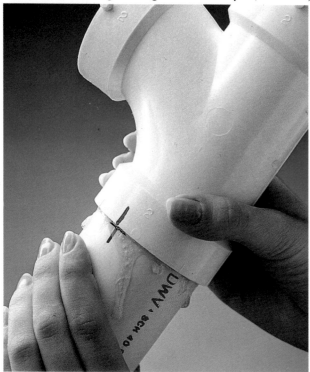

10 Spread solvent by twisting the pipe until marks are aligned. Hold pipe in place for about 20 seconds to prevent joint from slipping.

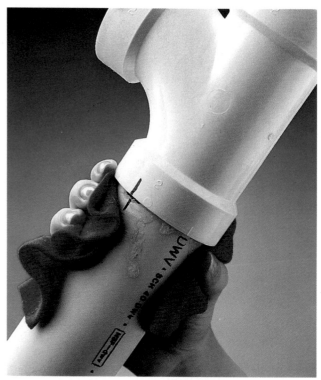

11 Wipe away excess solvent glue with a rag. Do not disturb joint for 30 minutes after gluing.

How to Cut & Fit Flexible Plastic Pipe

1 Cut flexible PB pipe with a plastic tubing cutter, available at home centers. (Flexible pipe also can be cut with a miter box or a sharp knife.) Remove any rough burrs with a utility knife.

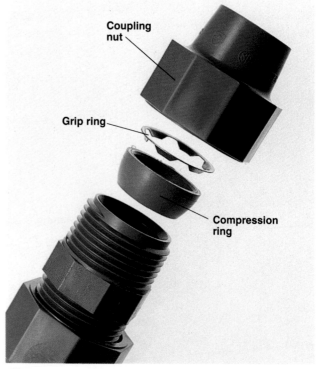

Coupling nut

Grip ring

Compression ring

2 Take each grip fitting apart and make sure that the grip ring and the compression ring or O-ring are positioned properly (page 103). Loosely reassemble the fitting.

108

3 Make a mark on the pipe showing the depth of the fitting socket, using a felt-tipped pen. Round off the edges of the pipe with emery cloth.

4 Lubricate the end of the pipe with petroleum jelly. Lubricated tip makes it easier to insert pipes into grip fittings.

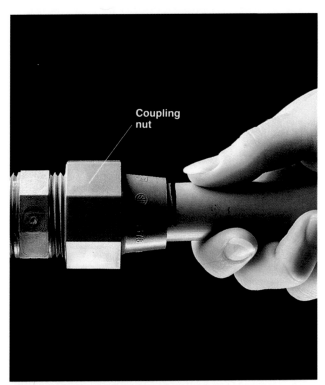

Coupling nut

5 Force end of pipe into fitting up to the mark on the pipe. Hand-tighten coupling nut.

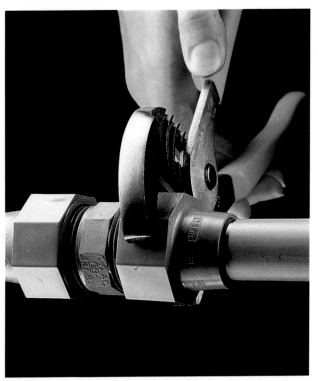

6 Tighten coupling nut about ½ turn with channel-type pliers. Turn on water and test the fitting. If the fitting leaks, tighten coupling nut slightly.

Working with Galvanized Iron

Galvanized iron pipe often is found in older homes, where it is used for water supply and small drain lines. It can be identified by the zinc coating that gives it a silver color, and by the threaded fittings used to connect pipes.

Galvanized iron pipes and fittings will corrode with age and eventually must be replaced. Low water pressure may be a sign that the insides of galvanized pipes have a buildup of rust. Blockage usually occurs in elbow fittings. Never try to clean the insides of galvanized iron pipes. Instead, remove and replace them as soon as possible.

Galvanized iron pipe and fittings are available at hardware stores and home improvement centers. Always specify the interior diameter (I.D.) when purchasing galvanized pipes and fittings. Pre-threaded pipes, called *nipples,* are available in lengths from 1" to 1 foot. If you need a longer length, have the store cut and thread the pipe to your dimensions.

Old galvanized iron can be difficult to repair. Fittings often are rusted in place, and what seems like a small job may become a large project. For example, cutting apart a section of pipe to replace a leaky fitting may reveal that adjacent pipes are also in need of replacement. If your job takes an unexpected amount of time, you can cap off any open lines and restore water to the rest of your house. Before you begin a repair, have on hand nipples and end caps that match your pipes.

Taking apart a system of galvanized iron pipes and fittings is time-consuming. Disassembly must start at the end of a pipe run, and each piece must be unscrewed before the next piece can be removed. Reaching the middle of a run to replace a section of pipe can be a long and tedious job. Instead, use a special three-piece fitting called a union. A union makes it possible to remove a section of pipe or a fitting without having to take the entire system apart.

Note: Galvanized iron is sometimes confused with "black iron." Both types have similar sizes and fittings. Black iron is used only for gas lines.

Measure old pipe. Include ½" at each end for the threaded portion of the pipe inside fitting. Bring overall measurement to the store when shopping for replacement parts.

Everything You Need:

Tools: tape measure, reciprocating saw with metal-cutting blade or a hacksaw, pipe wrenches, propane torch, wire brush.

Materials: nipples, end caps, union fitting, pipe joint compound, replacement fittings (if needed).

How to Remove & Replace a Galvanized Iron Pipe

1 Cut through galvanized iron pipe with a reciprocating saw and a metal-cutting blade, or with a hacksaw.

2 Hold fitting with one pipe wrench, and use another wrench to remove old pipe. Jaws of wrenches should face opposite directions. Always move wrench handle toward jaw opening.

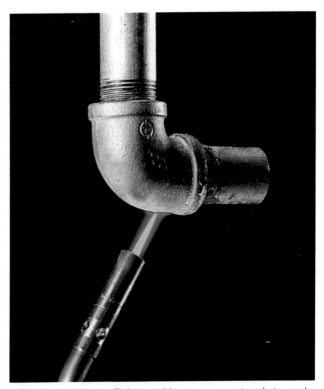

3 Remove any corroded fittings using two pipe wrenches. With jaws facing in opposite directions, use one wrench to turn fitting and the other to hold the pipe. Clean pipe threads with a wire brush.

4 Heat stubborn fittings with a propane torch to make them easier to remove. Apply flame for 5 to 10 seconds. Protect wood or other flammable materials from heat, using a double layer of sheet metal (page 92).

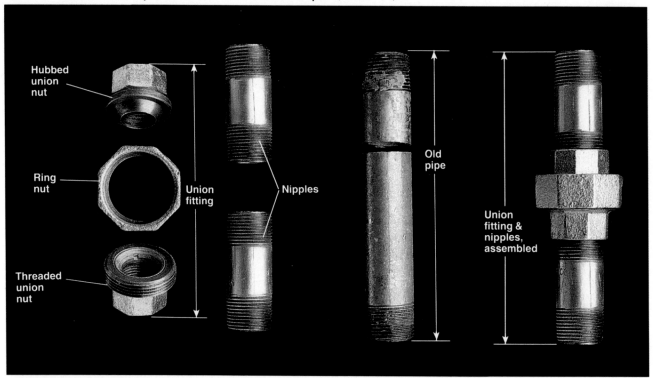

Hubbed union nut

Ring nut

Union fitting

Threaded union nut

Nipples

Old pipe

Union fitting & nipples, assembled

5 Replace a section of galvanized iron pipe with a union fitting and two threaded pipes (nipples). When assembled, the union and nipples must equal the length of the pipe that is being replaced.

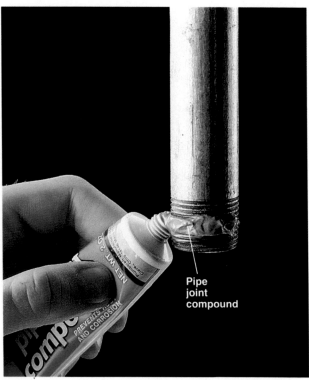

Pipe joint compound

6 Apply a bead of pipe joint compound around threaded ends of all pipes and nipples. Spread compound evenly over threads with fingertip.

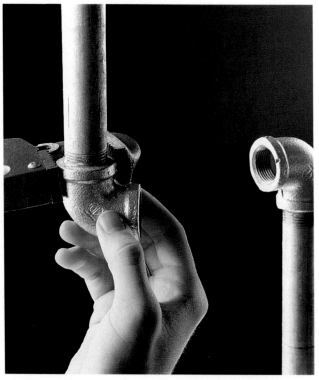

7 Screw new fittings onto pipe threads. Tighten fittings with two pipe wrenches, leaving them about ⅛ turn out of alignment to allow assembly of union.

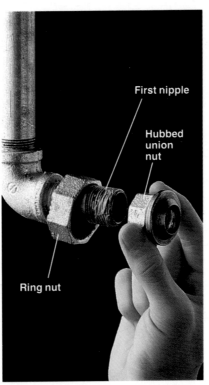

8 Screw first nipple into fitting, and tighten with pipe wrench.

9 Slide ring nut onto the installed nipple, then screw the hubbed union nut onto the nipple and tighten with a pipe wrench.

10 Screw second nipple onto other fitting. Tighten with pipe wrench.

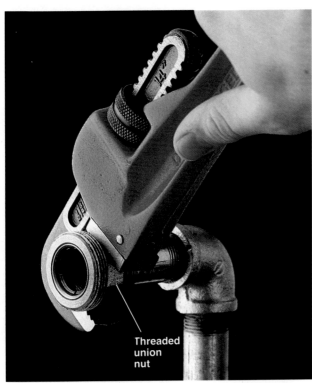

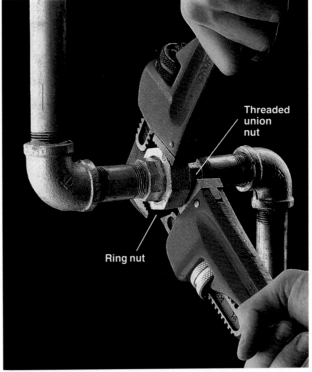

11 Screw threaded union nut onto second nipple. Tighten with a pipe wrench. Turn pipes into alignment, so that lip of hubbed union nut fits inside threaded union nut.

12 Complete the connection by screwing the ring nut onto the threaded union nut. Tighten ring nut with pipe wrenches.

Working with Cast Iron

Cast-iron pipe often is found in older homes, where it is used for large drain-waste-vent pipes, especially the main stack and sewer service lines. It can be identified by its dark color, rough surface, and large size. Cast-iron pipes in home drains usually are 3" or more in diameter.

Cast-iron pipes may rust through or hubbed fittings (below) may leak. If your house is more than 30 years old, you may find it necessary to replace a cast-iron pipe or joint.

Cast iron is heavy and difficult to cut and fit. One 5-ft. section of 4" pipe weighs 60 pounds. For this reason, leaky cast-iron pipe usually is replaced with a new plastic pipe of the same diameter. Plastic pipe can be joined to cast iron easily, using a banded coupling (below).

Cast iron is best cut with a rented tool called a *snap cutter.* Snap cutter designs vary, so follow the rental dealer's instructions for using the tool.

Everything You Need:

Tools: tape measure, chalk, adjustable wrenches, rented cast iron snap cutter (or hacksaw), ratchet wrench, screwdriver.

Materials: riser clamps or strap hangers, two wood blocks, 2½" wallboard screws, banded couplings, plastic replacement pipe.

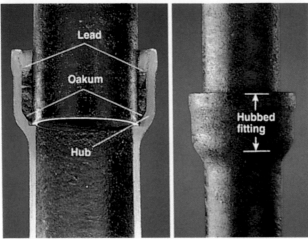

Hubbed fittings (shown cut away, left) may be used to join old cast-iron pipe. Hubbed pipe has a straight end and a flared end. The straight end of one pipe fits inside the hub of the next pipe. Joints are sealed with packing material (oakum) and lead. Repair leaky joints by cutting out the entire hubbed fitting and replacing with plastic pipe.

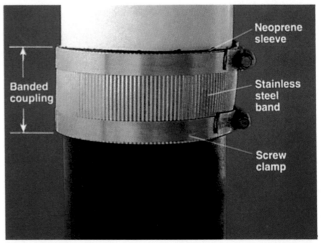

Banded couplings may be used to replace leaky cast-iron pipe with a PVC or ABS plastic pipe. The new plastic pipe is connected to the remaining cast-iron pipe with banded coupling. Banded coupling has a neoprene sleeve that seals the joint. Pipes are held together with stainless steel bands and screw clamps.

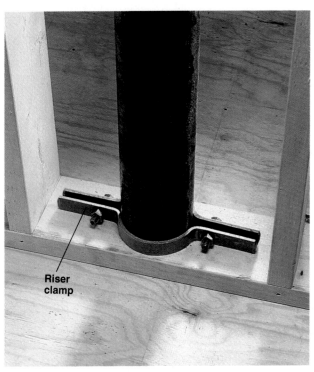

Before cutting a horizontal run of cast-iron drain pipe, make sure it is supported with strap hangers every 5 feet and at every joint connection.

Before cutting a vertical run of cast-iron pipe, make sure it is supported at every floor level with a riser clamp. Never cut apart pipe that is not supported.

How to Repair & Replace a Section of Cast-iron Pipe

1 Use chalk to mark cut lines on the cast-iron pipe. If replacing a leaky hub, mark at least 6" on each side of hub.

2 Support lower section of pipe by installing a riser clamp flush against bottom plate or floor.

3 Support upper section of pipe by installing a riser clamp 6" above pipe section to be replaced. Attach wood blocks to the studs with 2½" wallboard screws, so that the riser clamp rests on tops of blocks.

(continued next page)

How to Repair & Replace a Section of Cast-iron Pipe (continued)

4 Wrap chain of the cast iron cutter around the pipe, so that the cutting wheels are against chalk line.

5 Tighten the chain and snap the pipe according to the tool manufacturer's directions.

6 Repeat cutting at the other chalk line. Remove cut section of pipe.

7 Cut a length of PVC or ABS plastic pipe that is about 1″ shorter than section of cast-iron pipe that has been cut away.

Screw clamp

Banded coupling

Neoprene sleeve

8 Slip a banded coupling and a neoprene sleeve onto each end of the cast-iron pipe.

9 Make sure the cast-iron pipe is seated snugly against the rubber separator ring molded into the interior of the sleeve.

10 Fold back the end of each neoprene sleeve, until the molded separator ring on the inside of the sleeve is visible.

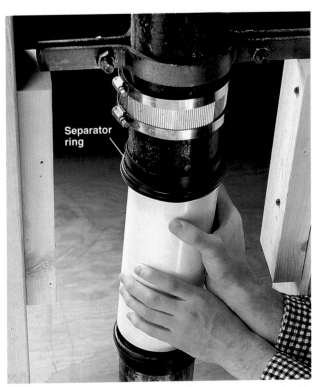

Separator ring

11 Position the new plastic pipe so it is aligned with the cast-iron pipes.

12 Roll the ends of the neoprene sleeves over the ends of the new plastic pipe.

13 Slide stainless steel bands and clamps over the neoprene sleeves.

14 Tighten the screw clamps with a ratchet wrench or screwdriver.

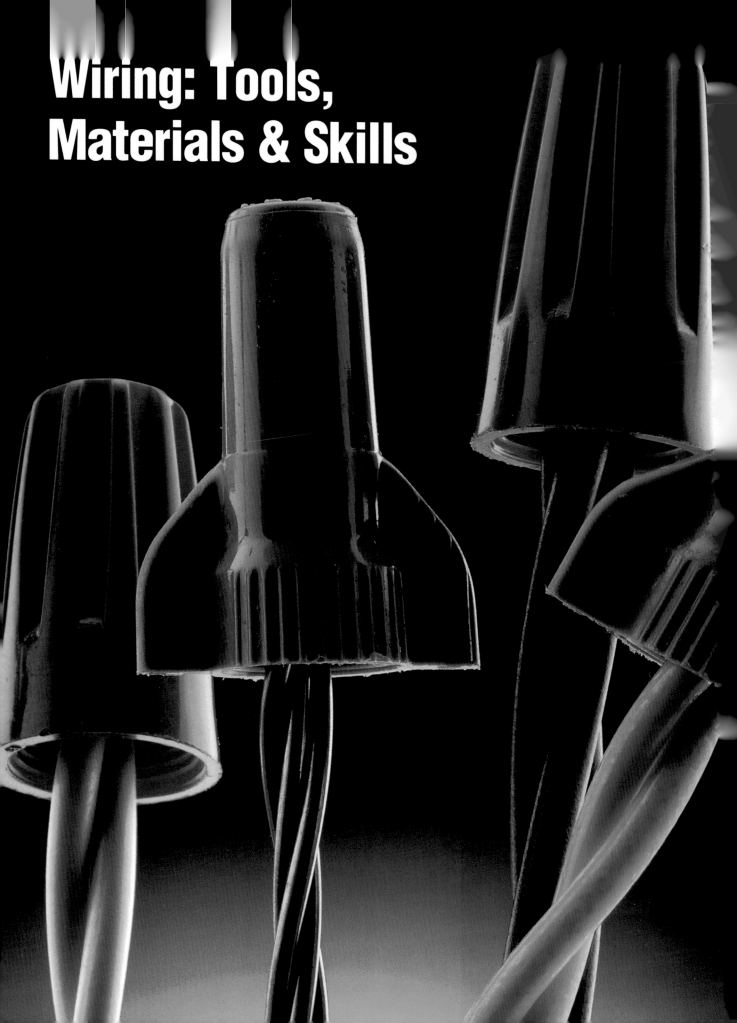

Wiring: Tools, Materials & Skills

2: Learn about Codes

To ensure public safety, your community requires that you get a permit to install new wiring and have the completed work reviewed by an appointed inspector. Electrical inspectors use the National Electrical Code (NEC) as the primary authority for evaluating wiring, but they also follow the local Building Code and Electrical Code standards.

As you begin planning new circuits, call or visit your local electrical inspector and discuss the project with him. The inspector can tell you which of the national and local Code requirements apply to your job, and may give you a packet of information summarizing these regulations. Later, when you apply to the inspector for a work permit, he will expect you to understand the local guidelines as well as a few basic National Electrical Code requirements.

The National Electrical Code is a set of standards that provides minimum safety requirements for wiring installations. It is revised every three years. The national Code requirements for the projects shown in this section are thoroughly explained on the following pages. For more information, you can find copies of the current NEC, as well as a number of excellent handbooks based on the NEC, at libraries and bookstores.

In addition to being the final authority on Code requirements, inspectors are electrical professionals with years of experience. Although they have busy schedules, most inspectors are happy to answer questions and help you design well-planned circuits.

Basic Electrical Code Requirements

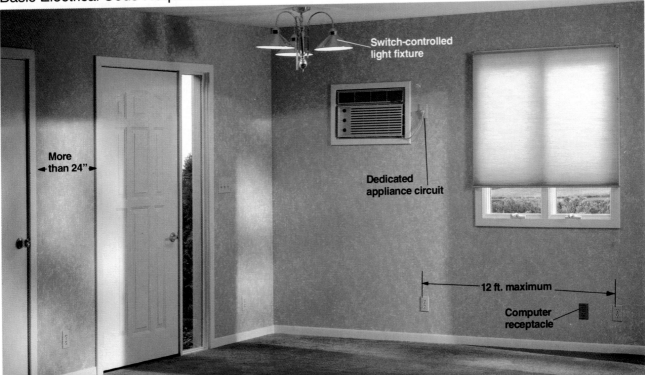

Electrical Code requirements for living areas:
Living areas need at least one 15-amp or 20-amp basic lighting/receptacle circuit for each 600 square feet of living space, and should have a "dedicated" circuit for each type of permanent appliance, like an air conditioner, computer, or a group of baseboard heaters. Receptacles on basic lighting/receptacle circuits should be spaced no more than 12 ft. apart. Many electricians and electrical inspectors recommend even closer spacing. Any wall more than 24" wide also needs a receptacle. Every room should have a wall switch that controls either a ceiling light or plug-in lamp.

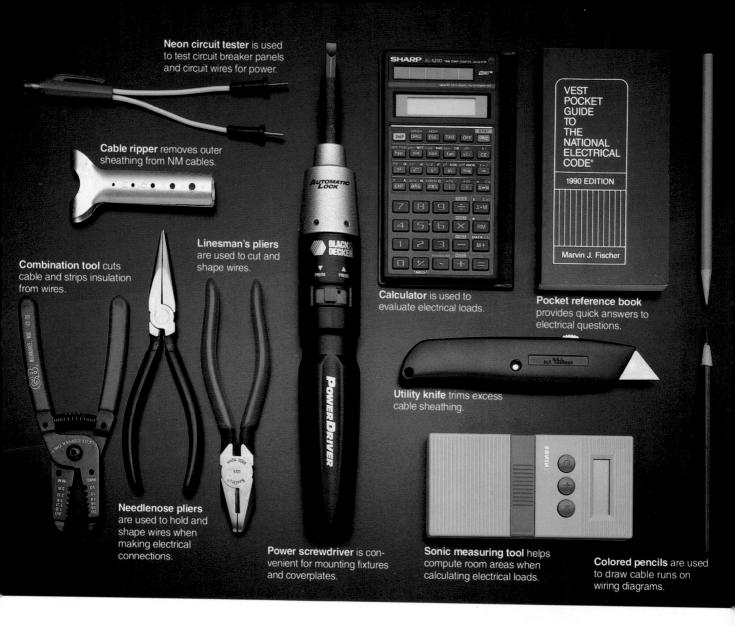

Neon circuit tester is used to test circuit breaker panels and circuit wires for power.

Cable ripper removes outer sheathing from NM cables.

Combination tool cuts cable and strips insulation from wires.

Linesman's pliers are used to cut and shape wires.

Calculator is used to evaluate electrical loads.

Pocket reference book provides quick answers to electrical questions.

Utility knife trims excess cable sheathing.

Needlenose pliers are used to hold and shape wires when making electrical connections.

Power screwdriver is convenient for mounting fixtures and coverplates.

Sonic measuring tool helps compute room areas when calculating electrical loads.

Colored pencils are used to draw cable runs on wiring diagrams.

VEST POCKET GUIDE TO THE NATIONAL ELECTRICAL CODE® 1990 EDITION — Marvin J. Fischer

SHARP EL-520D

Tools, Materials & Skills

To complete the wiring projects shown in this section, you need a few specialty electrical tools (above), as well as a basic collection of hand tools (page opposite). As with any tool purchase, invest in good-quality products when you buy tools for electrical work. Keep your tools clean, and sharpen or replace any cutting tools that have dull edges.

The materials used for electrical wiring have changed dramatically in the last 20 years, making it much easier for homeowners to do their own electrical work. The following pages show how to work with the following components:

- Electrical boxes (pages 122 to 127).
- Wires & cables (pages 128 to 137).
- Conduit (pages 138 to 141).
- Circuit breaker panels (pages 142 to 143).
- Connecting circuit breakers (pages 144 to 145).
- Circuit maps for 24 common wiring layouts (pages 146 to 157).

Plastic electrical boxes for indoor installations are ideal for do-it-yourself electrical work. They have preattached mounting nails for easy installation and are much less expensive than metal boxes.

Screwdrivers with insulated handles are used to assemble fixtures and make wire connections.

Tool belt keeps a wide variety of tools within easy reach.

Tape measure is used to position electrical boxes and determine cable lengths.

Nut driver and adjustable wrench are used to assemble and mount electrical fixtures.

Electrical tapes are used for marking wires and for attaching cables to a fish tape.

A fish tape is useful for installing cables in finished wall cavities and for pulling wires through conduit. Products designed for lubrication reduce friction and make it easier to pull cables and wires.

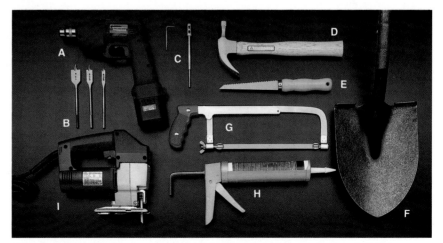

These basic tools are used for advanced wiring projects: drill (A), spade bits (B), and drill bit extension (C) for boring holes in framing members; hammer (D) for attaching electrical boxes; wallboard saw (E) for making cutouts in indoor walls; shovel (F) to dig trenches for outdoor wiring; hacksaw (G) for cutting conduit; caulk gun (H) for sealing gaps in exterior walls; jig saw (I) for making wall cutouts.

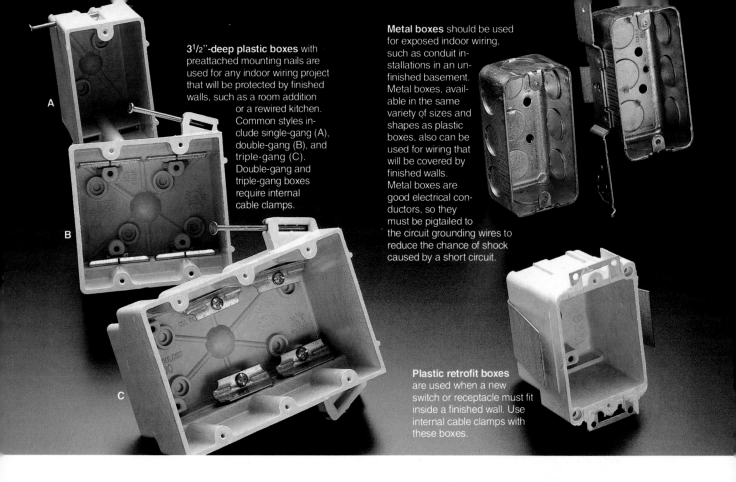

3¹/₂"-deep plastic boxes with preattached mounting nails are used for any indoor wiring project that will be protected by finished walls, such as a room addition or a rewired kitchen. Common styles include single-gang (A), double-gang (B), and triple-gang (C). Double-gang and triple-gang boxes require internal cable clamps.

Metal boxes should be used for exposed indoor wiring, such as conduit installations in an unfinished basement. Metal boxes, available in the same variety of sizes and shapes as plastic boxes, also can be used for wiring that will be covered by finished walls. Metal boxes are good electrical conductors, so they must be pigtailed to the circuit grounding wires to reduce the chance of shock caused by a short circuit.

Plastic retrofit boxes are used when a new switch or receptacle must fit inside a finished wall. Use internal cable clamps with these boxes.

Electrical Boxes

Use the chart below to select the proper type of box for your wiring project. For most indoor wiring done with NM cable, use plastic electrical boxes. Plastic boxes are inexpensive, lightweight, and easy to install.

Metal boxes also can be used for indoor NM cable installations and are still favored by some electricians, especially for supporting heavy ceiling light fixtures.

If you have a choice of box depths, always choose the deepest size available. Wire connections are easier to make if boxes are roomy.

Box type	Typical Uses
Plastic	• Protected indoor wiring, used with NM cable • Not suited for heavy light fixtures and fans
Metal	• Exposed indoor wiring, used with metal conduit • Protected indoor wiring, used with NM cable
Cast aluminum	• Outdoor wiring, used with metal conduit
PVC plastic	• Outdoor wiring, used with PVC conduit • Exposed indoor wiring, used with PVC conduit

Tips for Using Electrical Boxes

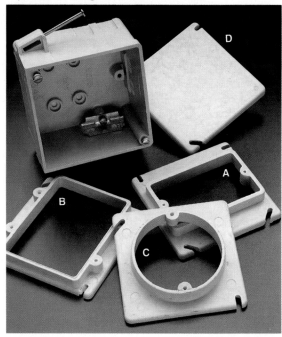

A square plastic box, 4" × 4" × 3" deep, provides extra space for making wire connections. It has preattached nails for easy mounting. A variety of adapter plates are available for 4" × 4" boxes, including single-gang (A), double-gang (B), light fixture (C), and junction box coverplate (D). Adapter plates come in several thicknesses to match different wall constructions.

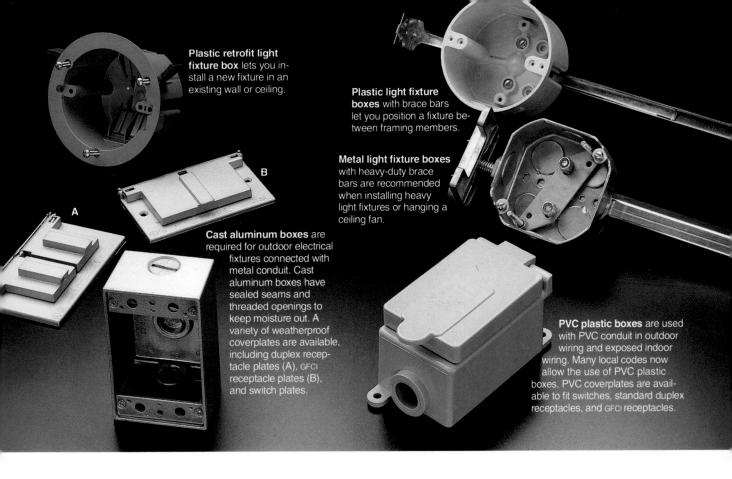

Plastic retrofit light fixture box lets you install a new fixture in an existing wall or ceiling.

Plastic light fixture boxes with brace bars let you position a fixture between framing members.

Metal light fixture boxes with heavy-duty brace bars are recommended when installing heavy light fixtures or hanging a ceiling fan.

Cast aluminum boxes are required for outdoor electrical fixtures connected with metal conduit. Cast aluminum boxes have sealed seams and threaded openings to keep moisture out. A variety of weatherproof coverplates are available, including duplex receptacle plates (A), GFCI receptacle plates (B), and switch plates.

PVC plastic boxes are used with PVC conduit in outdoor wiring and exposed indoor wiring. Many local codes now allow the use of PVC plastic boxes. PVC coverplates are available to fit switches, standard duplex receptacles, and GFCI receptacles.

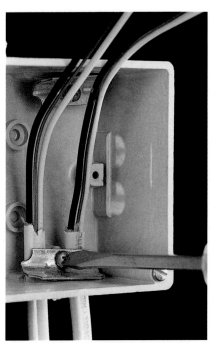

Boxes larger than 2" × 4", and all retrofit boxes, must have internal cable clamps. After installing cables in the box, tighten the cable clamps over the cables so they are gripped firmly, but not so tightly that the cable sheathing is crushed.

Metal boxes must be grounded to the circuit grounding system. Connect the circuit grounding wires to the box with a green insulated pigtail wire and wire nut (as shown) or with a grounding clip (page 138).

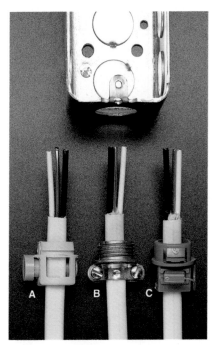

Cables entering a metal box must be clamped. A variety of clamps are available, including plastic clamps (A, C) and threaded metal clamps (B).

Installing Electrical Boxes

Install electrical boxes for receptacles, switches, and fixtures only after your wiring project plan has been approved by your inspector. Use your wiring plan as a guide, and follow electrical Code height and spacing guidelines when laying out box positions.

Always use the deepest electrical boxes that are practical for your installation. Using deep boxes ensures that you will meet Code regulations regarding box volume, and makes it easier to make the wire connections.

Some electrical fixtures, like recessed light fixtures, electric heaters, and exhaust fans, have built-in wire connection boxes. Install the frames for these fixtures at the same time you are installing the other electrical boxes.

Electrical boxes in adjacent rooms should be positioned close together when they share a common wall and are controlled by the same circuit. This simplifies the cable installations and also reduces the amount of cable needed.

Fixtures That Do Not Need Electrical Boxes

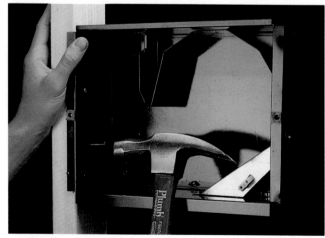

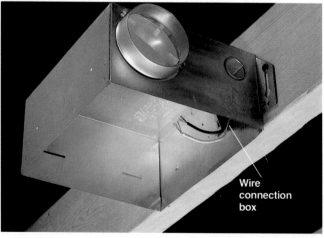

Wire connection box

Recessed fixtures that fit inside wall cavities have built-in wire connection boxes, and require no additional electrical boxes. Common recessed fixtures include electric blower-heaters (above, left), bathroom vent fans (above, right), and recessed light fixtures. Install the frames for these fixtures at the same time you are installing the other electrical boxes along the circuit. **Surface-mounted fixtures,** like electric baseboard heaters and under-cabinet fluorescent lights, also have built-in wire connection boxes. These fixtures are not installed until it is time to make the final hookups.

How to Install Electrical Boxes for Receptacles

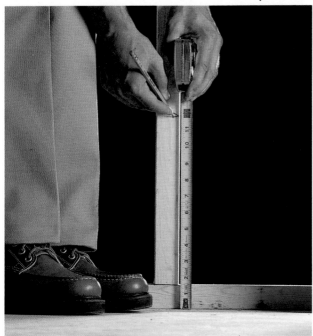

1 Mark the location of each box on studs. Standard receptacle boxes should be centered 12" above floor level. GFCI receptacle boxes in a bathroom should be mounted so they will be about 10" above the finished countertop.

2 Position each box against a stud so the front face will be flush with the finished wall. For example, if you will be installing 1/2" wallboard, position the box so it extends 1/2" past the face of the stud. Anchor the box by driving the mounting nails into the stud.

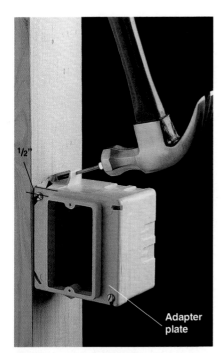

3 If installing 4" × 4" boxes, attach the adapter plates before positioning the boxes. Use adapter plates that match the thickness of the finished wall. Anchor the box by driving the mounting nails into the stud.

4 Open one knockout for each cable that will enter the box, using a hammer and screwdriver.

5 Break off any sharp edges that might damage vinyl cable sheathing by rotating a screwdriver in the knockout.

How to Install Boxes for Light Fixtures

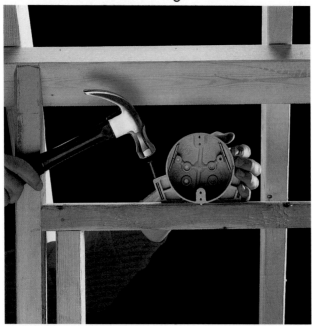

Position a light fixture box for a vanity light above the frame opening for a mirror or medicine cabinet. Place the box for a ceiling light fixture in the center of the room. The box for a stairway light should be mounted so every step will be lighted. Position each box against a framing member so the front face will be flush with the finished wall or ceiling, then anchor the box by driving the mounting nails into the framing member.

Attach a mounting strap to the box if one is required by the light-fixture manufacturer. Mounting straps are needed where the fixture mounting screws do not match the holes in the electrical box. A pre-attached grounding screw on the strap provides a place to pigtail grounding wires.

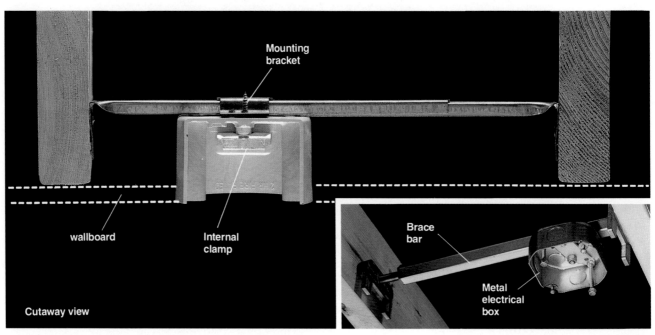

To position a light fixture between joists, attach an electrical box to an adjustable brace bar. Nail the ends of the brace bar to joists so the face of the box will be flush with the finished ceiling surface. Slide the box along the brace bar to the desired position,

then tighten the mounting screws. Use internal cable clamps when using a box with a brace bar. NOTE: For ceiling fans and heavy light fixtures, use a metal box and a heavy-duty brace bar rated for heavy loads (inset photo).

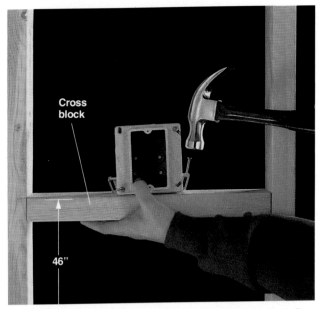

Install switch boxes at accessible locations, usually on the latch side of a door, with the center of the box 48" from the floor. In a bathroom or kitchen with partially tiled walls, switches are installed at 54" to 60" to keep them above the tile. The box for a thermostat is mounted at 48" to 60". Position each box against the side of a stud so the front face will be flush with the finished wall, and drive the mounting nails into the stud.

To install a switch box between studs, first install a cross block between studs, with the top edge 46" above the floor. Position the box on the cross block so the front face will be flush with the finished wall, and drive the mounting nails into the cross block.

How to Install Electrical Boxes to Match Finished Wall Depth

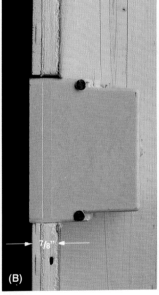

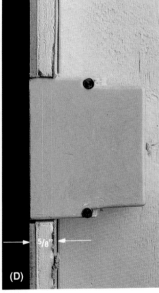

Consider the thickness of finished walls when mounting electrical boxes against framing members. Code requires that the front face of boxes be flush with the finished wall surface, so how you install boxes will vary depending on the type of wall finish that will be used. For example, if the walls will be finished with 1/2" wallboard (A), attach the boxes so the front faces extend 1/2" past the front of the framing members. With ceramic tile and wallboard (B), extend the boxes 7/8" past the framing members. With 1/4" Corian® over wallboard (C), boxes should extend 3/4"; and with wallboard and laminate (D), boxes extend 5/8".

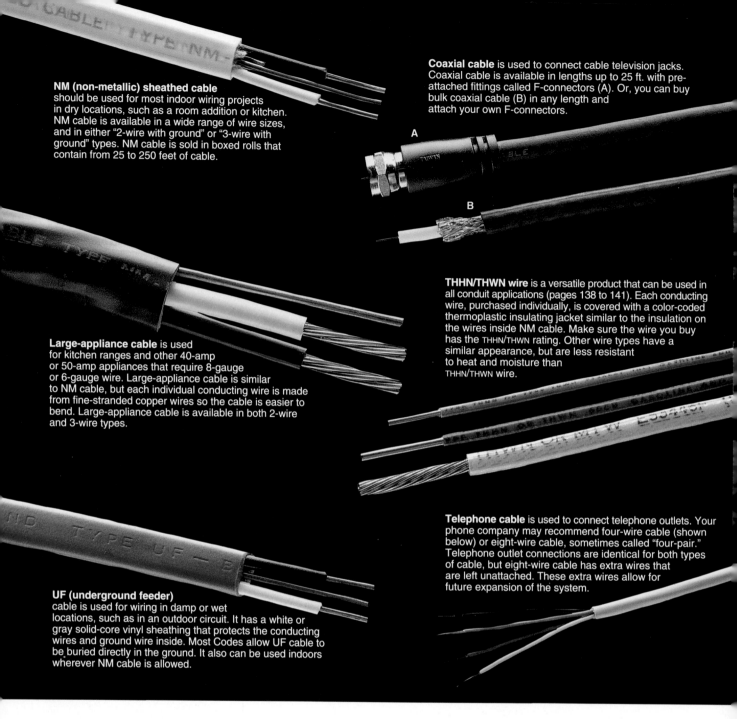

NM (non-metallic) sheathed cable
should be used for most indoor wiring projects
in dry locations, such as a room addition or kitchen.
NM cable is available in a wide range of wire sizes,
and in either "2-wire with ground" or "3-wire with
ground" types. NM cable is sold in boxed rolls that
contain from 25 to 250 feet of cable.

Coaxial cable is used to connect cable television jacks.
Coaxial cable is available in lengths up to 25 ft. with preattached fittings called F-connectors (A). Or, you can buy
bulk coaxial cable (B) in any length and
attach your own F-connectors.

A

B

Large-appliance cable is used
for kitchen ranges and other 40-amp
or 50-amp appliances that require 8-gauge
or 6-gauge wire. Large-appliance cable is similar
to NM cable, but each individual conducting wire is made
from fine-stranded copper wires so the cable is easier to
bend. Large-appliance cable is available in both 2-wire
and 3-wire types.

THHN/THWN wire is a versatile product that can be used in
all conduit applications (pages 138 to 141). Each conducting
wire, purchased individually, is covered with a color-coded
thermoplastic insulating jacket similar to the insulation on
the wires inside NM cable. Make sure the wire you buy
has the THHN/THWN rating. Other wire types have a
similar appearance, but are less resistant
to heat and moisture than
THHN/THWN wire.

Telephone cable is used to connect telephone outlets. Your
phone company may recommend four-wire cable (shown
below) or eight-wire cable, sometimes called "four-pair."
Telephone outlet connections are identical for both types
of cable, but eight-wire cable has extra wires that
are left unattached. These extra wires allow for
future expansion of the system.

UF (underground feeder)
cable is used for wiring in damp or wet
locations, such as in an outdoor circuit. It has a white or
gray solid-core vinyl sheathing that protects the conducting
wires and ground wire inside. Most Codes allow UF cable to
be buried directly in the ground. It also can be used indoors
wherever NM cable is allowed.

Wires & Cables

Many types of wire and cable are available at
home centers, but only a few are used in most
home wiring projects. Check your local Electrical Code to learn which type of wire to use, and
choose wire large enough for the circuit "ampacity" (page opposite). Cables are identified
by the wire gauge and number of *insulated* circuit wires they contain. In addition, all cables
have a grounding wire. For example, a cable
labeled "12/2 W G" contains two insulated 12-
gauge wires, plus a grounding wire.

Use NM cable for new wiring installed inside
walls. NM cable is easy to install when walls and
ceilings are unfinished; these techniques are
shown throughout this section. However, some
jobs require that you run cable through finished
walls, such as when you make the feeder cable
connection linking a new circuit to the circuit-
breaker panel. Running cable in finished walls
requires extra planning, and often is easier if you
work with a helper. Sometimes cables can be
run through a finished wall by using the gaps
around a chimney or plumbing soil stack. Other
techniques for running NM cable inside finished
walls are shown on pages 136 to 137.

Tips for Working with Wire

Wire gauge		Ampacity	Maximum wattage load
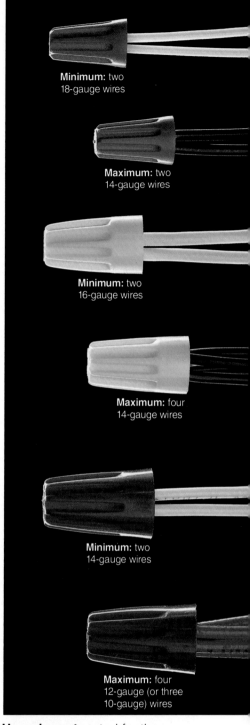	14-gauge	15 amps	1440 watts (120 volts)
	12-gauge	20 amps	1920 watts (120 volts) 3840 watts (240 volts)
	10-gauge	30 amps	2880 watts (120 volts) 5760 watts (240 volts)
	8-gauge	40 amps	7680 watts (240 volts)
	6-gauge	50 amps	9600 watts (240 volts)

Wire "ampacity" is a measurement of how much current a wire can carry safely. Ampacity varies according to the size of the wires, as shown above. When installing a new circuit , choose wire with an ampacity rating matching the circuit size. For dedicated appliance circuits, check the wattage rating of the appliance and make sure it does not exceed the maximum wattage load of the circuit.

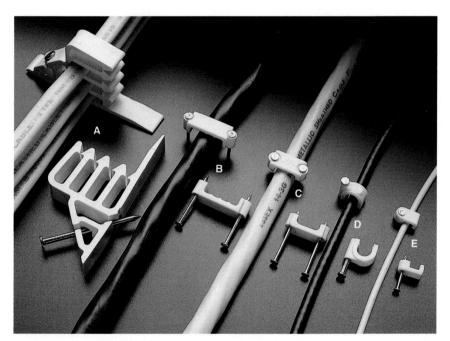

Use plastic cable staples to anchor cables to the sides of framing members. Choose staples sized to match the cables they anchor: Stack-It® staples (A) for attaching up to four 2-wire cables to the side of a framing member; 3/4" staples (B) for 12/2, 12/3, and all 10-gauge cables; 1/2" staples (C) for 14/2, 14/3, or 12/2 cables; coaxial staples (D) for anchoring television cables; bell wire staples (E) for attaching telephone cables. Cables should be anchored within 8" of each electrical box, and every 4 ft. thereafter.

Minimum: two 18-gauge wires

Maximum: two 14-gauge wires

Minimum: two 16-gauge wires

Maximum: four 14-gauge wires

Minimum: two 14-gauge wires

Maximum: four 12-gauge (or three 10-gauge) wires

Use wire nuts rated for the wires you are connecting. Wire nuts are color-coded by size, but the coding scheme varies according to manufacturer. The wire nuts shown above come from one major manufacturer. To ensure safe connections, each wire nut is rated for both minimum and maximum wire capacity. These wire nuts can be used to connect both conducting wires and grounding wires. Green wire nuts are used only for grounding wires.

How to Connect Wires to Screw Terminals

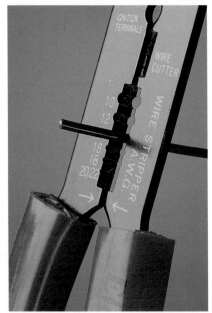

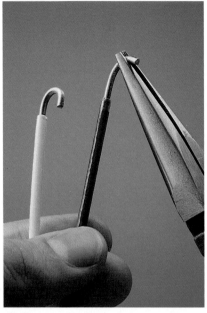

1 Strip about ¾" of insulation from each wire, using a combination tool. Choose the stripper opening that matches the gauge of the wire, then clamp wire in tool. Pull the wire firmly to remove plastic insulation.

2 Form a C-shaped loop in the end of each wire, using a needle-nose pliers. The wire should have no scratches or nicks.

3 Hook each wire around the screw terminal so it forms a clockwise loop. Tighten screw firmly. Insulation should just touch head of screw. Never place the ends of two wires under a single screw terminal. Instead, use a pigtail wire (page opposite).

How to Connect Wires with Push-in Fittings

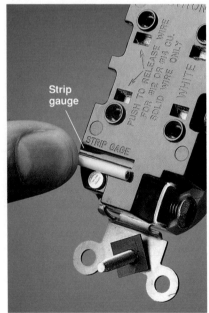

1 Mark the amount of insulation to be stripped from each wire, using the strip gauge on the back of the switch or receptacle. Strip the wires using a combination tool (step 1, above). Never use push-in fittings with aluminum wiring.

2 Insert the bare copper wires firmly into the push-in fittings on the back of the switch or receptacle. When inserted, wires should have no bare copper exposed.

Remove a wire from a push-in fitting by inserting a small nail or screwdriver in the release opening next to the wire. Wire will pull out easily.

How to Connect Two or More Wires with a Wire Nut

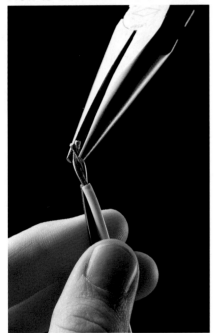

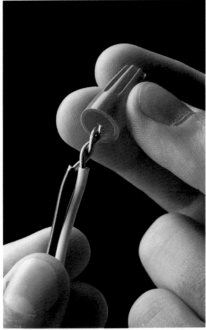

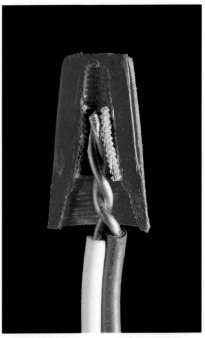

1 Strip about ½" of insulation from each wire. Hold the wires parallel, and twist them together in a clockwise direction, using a needle-nose pliers or combination tool.

2 Screw the wire nut onto the twisted wires. Tug gently on each wire to make sure it is secure. In a proper connection, no bare wire should be exposed past the bottom of the wire nut.

Wire nut (shown in cutaway) has metal threads that grip the bare ends of the wires. When connected, the wire nut should completely cover the bare wires.

How to Pigtail Two or More Wires

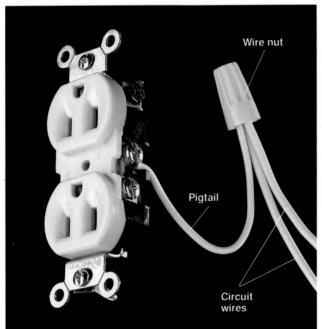

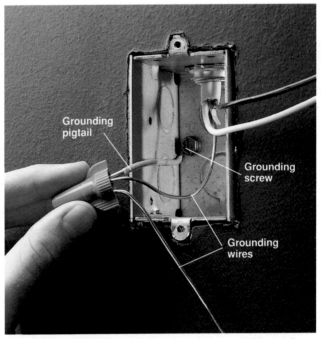

Connect two or more wires to a single screw terminal with a pigtail. A pigtail is a short piece of wire. One end of the pigtail connects to a screw terminal, and the other end connects to circuit wires, using a wire nut. A pigtail also can be used to lengthen circuit wires that are too short.

Grounding pigtail has green insulation, and is available with a preattached grounding screw. This grounding screw connects to the grounded metal electrical box. The end of the pigtail wire connects to the bare copper grounding wires with a wire nut.

131

Installing NM Cable

NM cable is used for all indoor wiring projects except those requiring conduit (see pages 138 to 141). Cut and install the cable after all electrical boxes have been mounted. Refer to your wiring plan to make sure each length of cable is correct for the circuit size and configuration.

Cable runs are difficult to measure exactly, so leave plenty of extra wire when cutting each length. Cable splices inside walls are not allowed by Code. When inserting cables into a circuit breaker panel, **make sure the power is shut off** (page 144).

After all cables are installed, call your electrical inspector to arrange for the rough-in inspection. Do not install wallboard or attach light fixtures and other devices until this inspection is done.

Everything You Need:

Tools: drill, bits, tape measure, cable ripper, combination tool, screwdrivers, needlenose pliers, hammer.

Materials: NM cable, cable clamps, cable staples, masking tape, grounding pigtails, wire nuts.

Pulling cables through studs is easier if you drill smooth, straight holes at the same height. Prevent kinks by straightening the cable before pulling it through the studs.

How to Install NM Cable

1 Drill ⁵/₈" holes in framing members for the cable runs. This is done easily with a right-angle drill, available at rental centers. Holes should be set back at least 1¹/₄" from the front face of the framing members.

2 Where cables will turn corners (step 6, page opposite), drill intersecting holes in adjoining faces of studs. Measure and cut all cables, allowing 2 ft. extra at ends entering breaker panel, and 1 ft. for ends entering electrical box.

3 Shut off power to circuit breaker panel (page 144). Use a cable ripper to strip cable, leaving at least ¼" of sheathing to enter the circuit breaker panel. Clip away the excess sheathing.

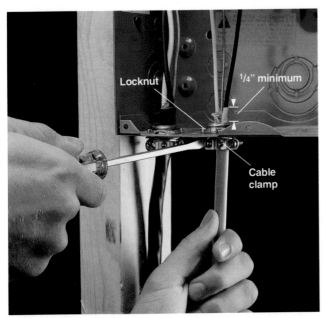

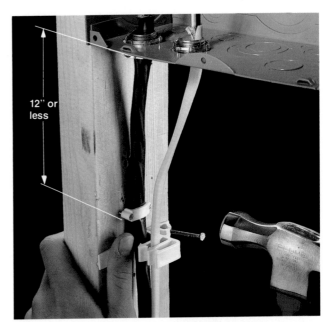

4 Open a knockout in the circuit breaker panel, using a hammer and screwdriver. Insert a cable clamp into the knockout, and secure it with a locknut. Insert the cable though the clamp so that at least 1/4" of sheathing extends inside the circuit breaker panel. Tighten the mounting screws on the clamp so the cable is gripped securely, but not so tightly that the sheathing is crushed.

5 Anchor the cable to the center of a framing member within 12" of the circuit breaker panel, using a cable staple. Stack-It® staples work well where two or more cables must be anchored to the same side of a stud. Run the cable to the first electrical box. Where the cable runs along the sides of framing members, anchor it with cable staples no more than 4 ft. apart.

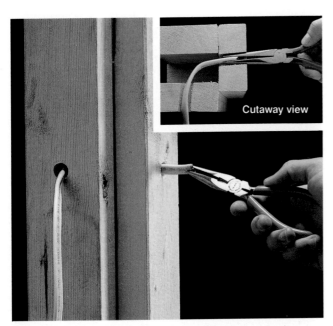

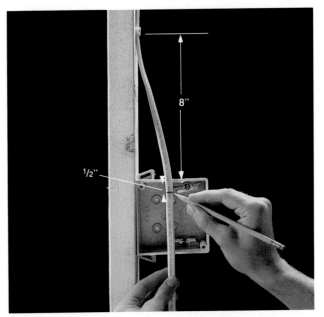

6 At corners, form a slight L-shaped bend in the end of the cable and insert it into one hole. Retrieve cable through the other hole, using needlenose pliers (inset).

7 At the electrical box, staple the cable to a framing member 8" from the box. Hold the cable taut against the front of the box, and mark a point on the sheathing 1/2" past the box edge. Strip cable from the marked line to the end, using a cable ripper, and clip away excess sheathing with a combination tool. Insert the cable through the knockout in the box.

(continued next page)

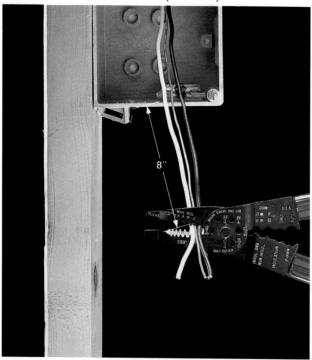

8 As each cable is installed in a box, clip back each wire so that 8" of workable wire extends past the front edge of the box.

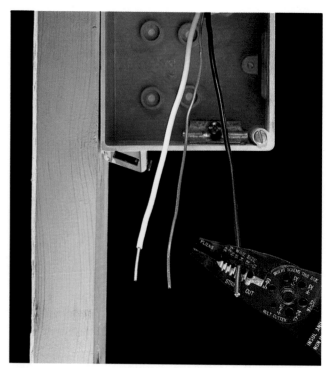

9 Strip ³/4" of insulation from each circuit wire in the box, using a combination tool. Take care not to nick the copper.

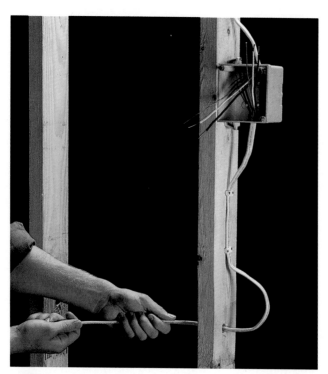

10 Continue the circuit by running cable between each pair of electrical boxes, leaving an extra 1 ft. of cable at each end.

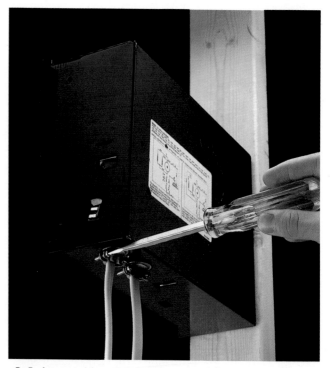

11 At metal boxes and recessed fixtures, open knockouts and attach cables with cable clamps. From inside fixture, strip away all but ¹/4" of sheathing. Clip back wires so there is 8" of workable length, then strip ³/4" of insulation from each wire.

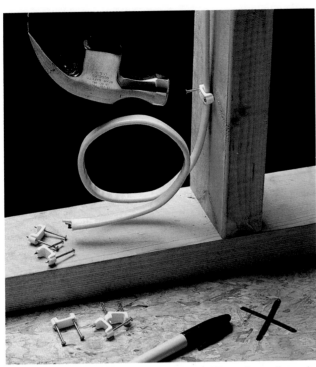

12 For a surface-mounted fixture like a baseboard heater or fluorescent light fixture, staple the cable to a stud near the fixture location, leaving plenty of excess cable. Mark the floor so the cable will be easy to find after the walls are finished.

13 At each recessed fixture and metal electrical box, connect one end of a grounding pigtail to the metal frame, using a rounding clip attached to the frame (shown above) or a green grounding screw (page 138).

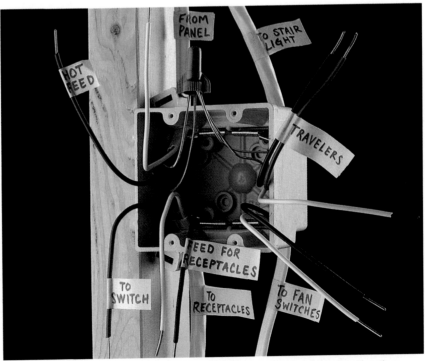

14 At each electrical box and recessed fixture, join the grounding wires together with a wire nut. If box has internal clamps, tighten the clamps over the cables.

15 Label the cables entering each box to indicate their destinations. In boxes with complex wiring configurations, also tag the individual wires to make final hookups easier. After all cables are installed, your rough-in work is ready to be reviewed by the electrical inspector.

135

How to Run NM Cable Inside a Finished Wall

  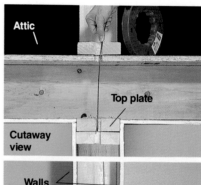

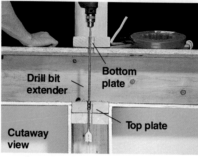 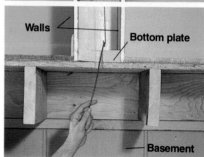

1 From the unfinished space below the finished wall, look for a reference point, like a soil stack, plumbing pipes, or electrical cables, that indicates the location of the wall above. Choose a location for the new cable that does not interfere with existing utilities. Drill a 1" hole up into the stud cavity.

2 From the unfinished space above the finished wall, find the top of the stud cavity by measuring from the same fixed reference point used in step 1. Drill a 1" hole down through the top plate and into the stud cavity, using a drill bit extender.

3 Extend a fish tape down through the top plate, twisting the tape until it reaches the bottom of the stud cavity. From the unfinished space below the wall, use a piece of stiff wire with a hook on one end to retrieve the fish tape through the drilled hole in the bottom plate.

4 Trim back 3" of outer insulation from the end of the NM cable, then insert the wires through the loop at the tip of the fish tape.

5 Bend the wires against the cable, then use electrical tape to bind them tightly. Apply cable-pulling lubricant to the taped end of the fish tape.

6 From above the finished wall, pull steadily on the fish tape to draw the cable up through the stud cavity. This job will be easier if you have a helper feed the cable from below as you pull.

Tips for Running Cable Inside Finished Walls

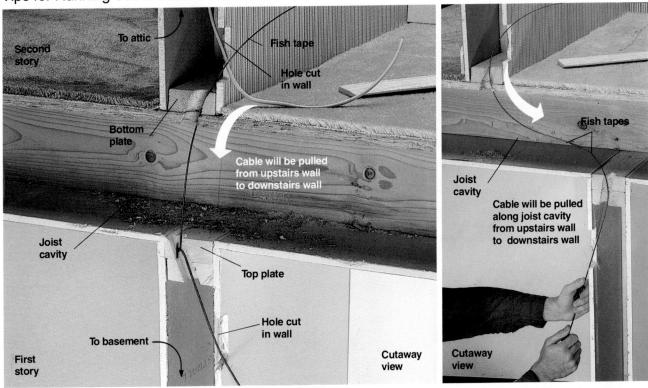

Second story

To attic

Fish tape

Hole cut in wall

Bottom plate

Cable will be pulled from upstairs wall to downstairs wall

Joist cavity

Top plate

Hole cut in wall

To basement

First story

Cutaway view

Fish tapes

Joist cavity

Cable will be pulled along joist cavity from upstairs wall to downstairs wall

Cutaway view

If there is no access space above and below a wall (page opposite), cut openings in the finished walls to run a cable. This often occurs in two-story homes when a cable is extended from an upstairs wall to a downstairs wall. Cut small openings in the wall near the top and bottom plates, then drill an angled 1" hole through each plate. Extend a fish tape into the joist cavity between the walls and use it to pull the cable from one wall to the next. If the walls line up one over the other (left), you can retrieve the fish tape using a piece of stiff wire. If walls do not line up (right), use a second fish tape. After running the cable, repair the holes in the walls with patching plaster, or wallboard scraps and taping compound.

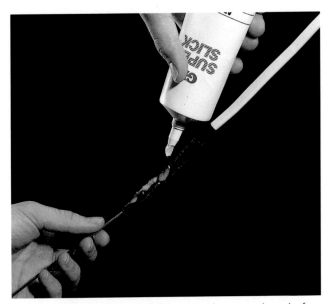

Apply cable-pulling lubricant to the taped end of the fish tape when a cable must be pulled through a sharp bend. Do not use oil or petroleum jelly as a lubricant, because they can damage the thermoplastic cable sheathing.

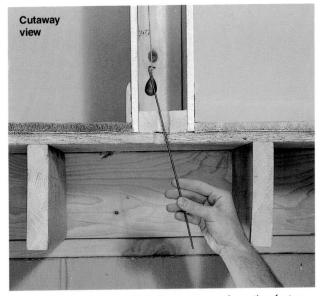

Cutaway view

If you do not have a fish tape, use a length of sturdy mason's string and a lead fishing weight or heavy washer to fish down through a stud cavity. Drop the line into the stud cavity from above, then use a piece of stiff wire to hook the line from below.

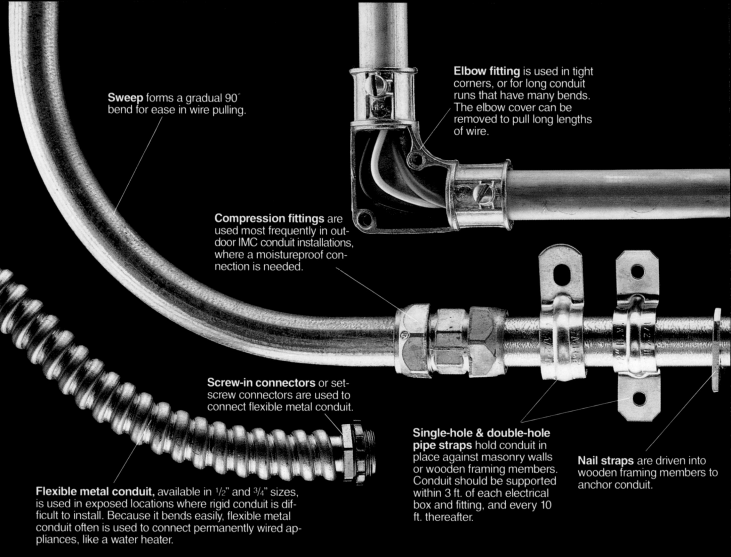

Sweep forms a gradual 90° bend for ease in wire pulling.

Elbow fitting is used in tight corners, or for long conduit runs that have many bends. The elbow cover can be removed to pull long lengths of wire.

Compression fittings are used most frequently in outdoor IMC conduit installations, where a moistureproof connection is needed.

Screw-in connectors or set-screw connectors are used to connect flexible metal conduit.

Flexible metal conduit, available in ¹/₂" and ³/₄" sizes, is used in exposed locations where rigid conduit is difficult to install. Because it bends easily, flexible metal conduit often is used to connect permanently wired appliances, like a water heater.

Single-hole & double-hole pipe straps hold conduit in place against masonry walls or wooden framing members. Conduit should be supported within 3 ft. of each electrical box and fitting, and every 10 ft. thereafter.

Nail straps are driven into wooden framing members to anchor conduit.

Conduit

Electrical wiring that runs in exposed locations must be protected by rigid tubing, called conduit. For example, conduit is used for wiring that runs across masonry walls in a basement laundry, and for exposed outdoor wiring. THHN/THWN wire (page 128) normally is installed inside conduit, although UF or NM cable also can be installed in conduit.

There are several types of conduit available, so check with your electrical inspector to find out which type meets Code requirements in your area. Conduit installed outdoors must be rated for exterior use. Metal conduit should be used only with metal boxes, never with plastic boxes.

At one time, conduit could only be fitted by using elaborate bending techniques and special tools. Now, however, a variety of shaped fittings are available to let a homeowner join conduit easily.

Electrical Grounding in Metal Conduit

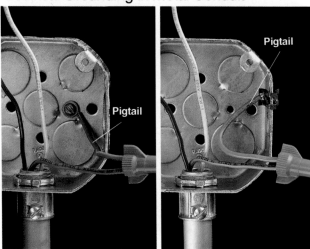

Pigtail

Pigtail

Install a green insulated grounding wire for any circuit that runs through metal conduit. Although the Code allows the metal conduit to serve as the grounding conductor, most electricians install a green insulated wire as a more dependable means of grounding the system. The grounding wires must be connected to metal boxes with a pigtail and grounding screw (left) or grounding clip (right).

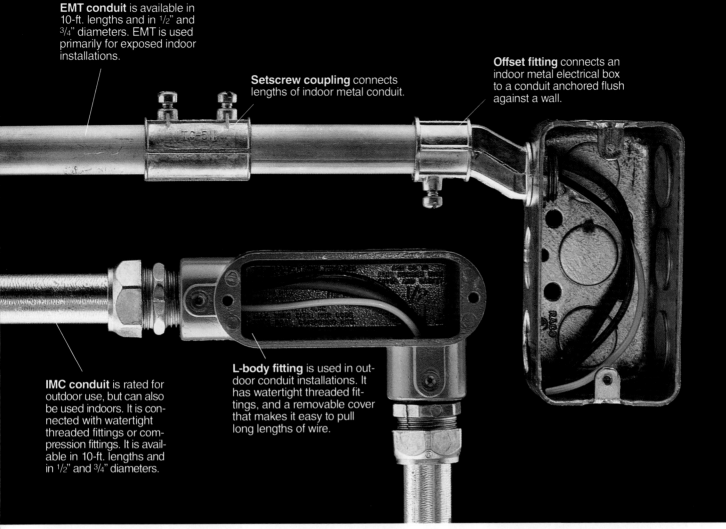

EMT conduit is available in 10-ft. lengths and in 1/2" and 3/4" diameters. EMT is used primarily for exposed indoor installations.

Setscrew coupling connects lengths of indoor metal conduit.

Offset fitting connects an indoor metal electrical box to a conduit anchored flush against a wall.

IMC conduit is rated for outdoor use, but can also be used indoors. It is connected with watertight threaded fittings or compression fittings. It is available in 10-ft. lengths and in 1/2" and 3/4" diameters.

L-body fitting is used in outdoor conduit installations. It has watertight threaded fittings, and a removable cover that makes it easy to pull long lengths of wire.

Wire Capacities of Conduit

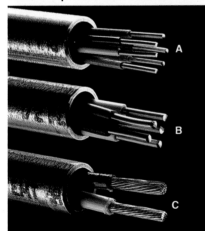

Conduit 1/2" in diameter can hold up to six 14-gauge or 12-gauge THHN/THWN wires (A), five 10-gauge wires (B), or two 8-gauge wires (C). Use 3/4" conduit if the number of wires exceeds this capacity.

Three Metal Conduit Variations

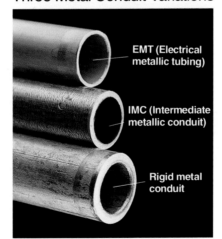

EMT (Electrical metallic tubing)

IMC (Intermediate metallic conduit)

Rigid metal conduit

EMT is lightweight and easy to install, but should not be used where it can be damaged. IMC has thicker, galvanized walls and is a good choice for exposed outdoor use. Rigid metal conduit provides the greatest protection for wires, but is more expensive and requires threaded fittings.

Plastic Conduit Variation

Plastic PVC conduit is allowed by many local Codes. It is assembled with solvent glue and PVC fittings that resemble those for metal conduit. PVC conduit should be attached only to PVC boxes, never to metal boxes. When wiring with PVC conduit, always run a green grounding wire.

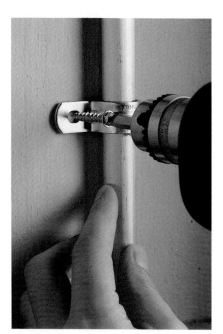

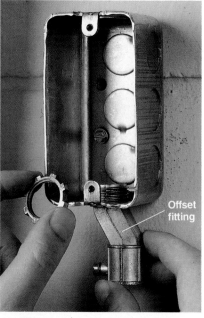

1 Measure from floor to position electrical boxes on wall, and mark location for mounting screws. Boxes for receptacles in an unfinished basement or other damp area are mounted at least 2 ft. from the floor. Laundry receptacles usually are mounted at 48".

2 Drill pilot holes with a masonry bit, then mount the boxes against masonry walls with Tapcon® anchors. Or, use masonry anchors and pan-head screws.

3 Open one knockout for each length of conduit that will be attached to the box. Attach an offset fitting to each knockout, using a locknut.

Offset fitting

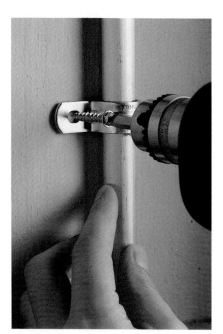

4 Measure the first length of conduit and cut it with a hacksaw. Remove any rough inside edges with a pipe reamer or a round file. Attach the conduit to the offset fitting on the box, and tighten the setscrew.

5 Anchor the conduit against the wall with pipe straps and Tapcon® anchors. Conduit should be anchored within 3 ft. of each box and fitting, and every 10 ft. thereafter.

6 Make conduit bends by attaching a sweep fitting, using a setscrew fitting or compression fitting. Continue conduit run by attaching additional lengths, using setscrew or compression fittings.

7 Use an elbow fitting in conduit runs that have many bends, or runs that require very long wires. The cover on the elbow fitting can be removed to make it easier to extend a fish tape and pull wires.

8 At the service breaker panel, **turn the power OFF, then remove the cover and test for power** (page 144). Open a knockout in the panel, then attach a set-screw fitting and install the last length of conduit.

9 Unwind the fish tape and extend it through the conduit from the circuit breaker panel outward. Remove the cover on an elbow fitting when extending the fish tape around tight corners.

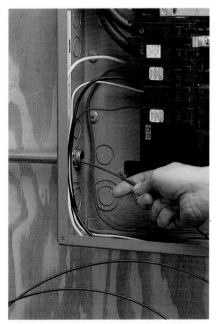

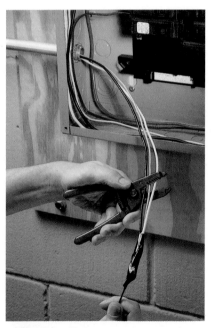

10 Insert the wires through the loop at the end of the fish tape, and wrap them with electrical tape. Straighten the wires to prevent kinks, and apply wire-pulling lubricant to the taped end of the fish tape.

11 Retrieve the wires through the conduit by pulling on the fish tape with steady pressure. **NOTE: Use extreme care** when using a metal fish tape inside a circuit breaker panel, even when the power is turned OFF.

12 Clip off the taped ends of the wires. Leave 2 ft. of wire at the service panel, and 8" at each electrical box.

Circuit Breaker Panels

The circuit breaker panel is the electrical distribution center for your home. It divides the current into branch circuits that are carried throughout the house. Each branch circuit is controlled by a circuit breaker that protects the wires from dangerous current overloads. When installing new circuits, the last step is to connect the wires to new circuit breakers at the panel. Working inside a circuit breaker panel is not dangerous if you follow basic safety procedures. Always shut off the main circuit breaker and test for power be-

fore touching any parts inside the panel, and **never touch the service wire lugs.** If unsure of your own skills, hire an electrician to make the final circuit connections. (If you have an older electrical service with fuses instead of circuit breakers, always have an electrician make these final hookups.)

If the main circuit breaker panel does not have enough open slots to hold new circuit breakers, install a subpanel. This job is well within the skill level

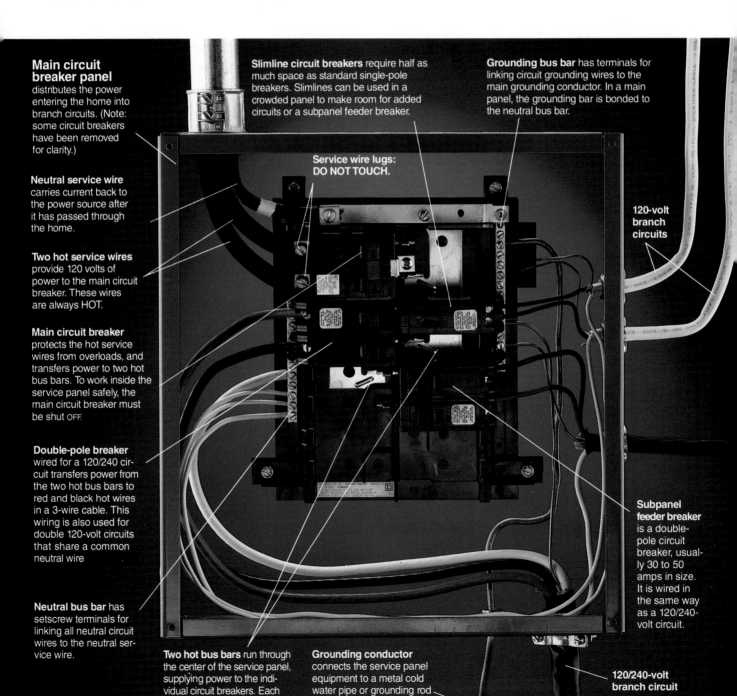

Main circuit breaker panel distributes the power entering the home into branch circuits. (Note: some circuit breakers have been removed for clarity.)

Neutral service wire carries current back to the power source after it has passed through the home.

Two hot service wires provide 120 volts of power to the main circuit breaker. These wires are always HOT.

Main circuit breaker protects the hot service wires from overloads, and transfers power to two hot bus bars. To work inside the service panel safely, the main circuit breaker must be shut OFF.

Double-pole breaker wired for a 120/240 circuit transfers power from the two hot bus bars to red and black hot wires in a 3-wire cable. This wiring is also used for double 120-volt circuits that share a common neutral wire

Neutral bus bar has setscrew terminals for linking all neutral circuit wires to the neutral service wire.

Slimline circuit breakers require half as much space as standard single-pole breakers. Slimlines can be used in a crowded panel to make room for added circuits or a subpanel feeder breaker.

Service wire lugs: DO NOT TOUCH.

Grounding bus bar has terminals for linking circuit grounding wires to the main grounding conductor. In a main panel, the grounding bar is bonded to the neutral bus bar.

120-volt branch circuits

Subpanel feeder breaker is a double-pole circuit breaker, usually 30 to 50 amps in size. It is wired in the same way as a 120/240-volt circuit.

Two hot bus bars run through the center of the service panel, supplying power to the individual circuit breakers. Each carries 120 volts of power

Grounding conductor connects the service panel equipment to a metal cold water pipe or grounding rod driven into the earth

120/240-volt branch circuit

of an experienced do-it-yourselfer, although you can also hire an electrician to install the subpanel.

Before installing any new wiring, evaluate your electrical service to make sure it provides enough current to support both the existing wiring and any new circuits. If your service does not provide enough power, have an electrician upgrade it to a higher amp rating. During the upgrade, the electrician will install a new circuit breaker panel with enough extra breaker slots for the new circuits you want to install.

Safety Warning:

Never touch any parts inside a circuit breaker panel until you have checked for power (page 144). Circuit breaker panels differ in appearance, depending on the manufacturer. Never begin work in a circuit breaker panel until you understand its layout and can identify the parts.

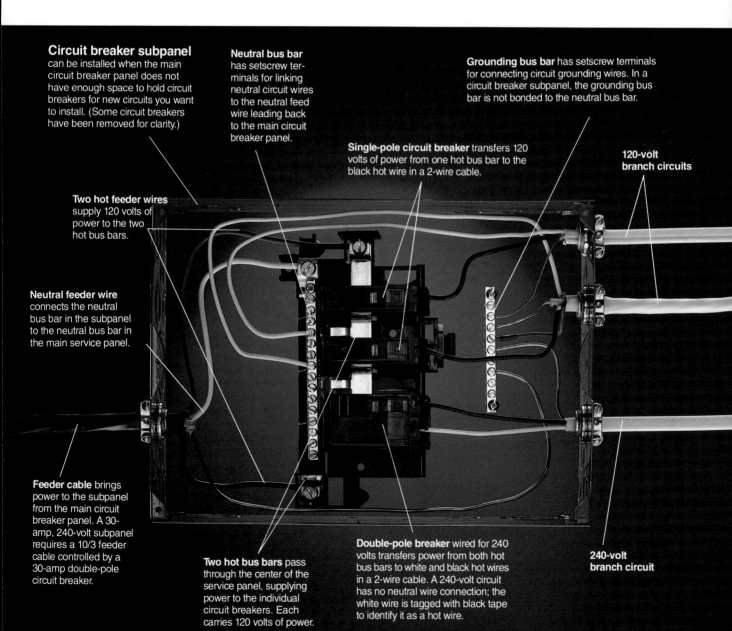

Circuit breaker subpanel can be installed when the main circuit breaker panel does not have enough space to hold circuit breakers for new circuits you want to install. (Some circuit breakers have been removed for clarity.)

Neutral bus bar has setscrew terminals for linking neutral circuit wires to the neutral feed wire leading back to the main circuit breaker panel.

Grounding bus bar has setscrew terminals for connecting circuit grounding wires. In a circuit breaker subpanel, the grounding bus bar is not bonded to the neutral bus bar.

Single-pole circuit breaker transfers 120 volts of power from one hot bus bar to the black hot wire in a 2-wire cable.

120-volt branch circuits

Two hot feeder wires supply 120 volts of power to the two hot bus bars.

Neutral feeder wire connects the neutral bus bar in the subpanel to the neutral bus bar in the main service panel.

Feeder cable brings power to the subpanel from the main circuit breaker panel. A 30-amp, 240-volt subpanel requires a 10/3 feeder cable controlled by a 30-amp double-pole circuit breaker.

Two hot bus bars pass through the center of the service panel, supplying power to the individual circuit breakers. Each carries 120 volts of power.

Double-pole breaker wired for 240 volts transfers power from both hot bus bars to white and black hot wires in a 2-wire cable. A 240-volt circuit has no neutral wire connection; the white wire is tagged with black tape to identify it as a hot wire.

240-volt branch circuit

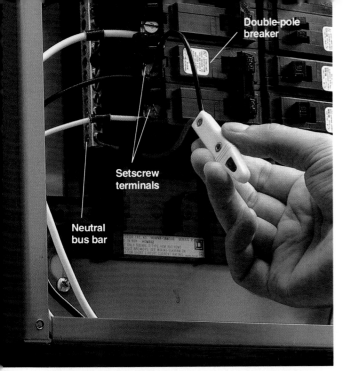

Double-pole breaker

Setscrew terminals

Neutral bus bar

Connecting Circuit Breakers

The last step in a wiring project is connecting circuits at the breaker panel. After this is done, the work is ready for the final inspection.

Circuits are connected at the main breaker panel, if it has enough open slots, or at a circuit breaker sub-panel. When working at a subpanel, make sure the feeder breaker at the main panel has been turned OFF, and test for power (photo, left) before touching any parts in the subpanel.

Make sure the circuit breaker amperage does not exceed the "ampacity" of the circuits wire you are connecting to it (page 129). Also be aware that circuit breaker styles and installation techniques vary according to manufacturer. Use breakers designed for your type of panel.

Test for current before touching any parts inside a circuit breaker panel. With main breaker turned OFF but all other breakers turned ON, touch one probe of a neon tester to the neutral bus bar, and touch other probe to each setscrew on one of the double-pole breakers (not the main breaker). If tester does not light for either setscrew, it is safe to work in the panel.

Everything You Need:

Tools: screwdriver, hammer, pencil, combination tool, cable ripper, neon circuit tester, pliers.

Materials: cable clamps, single- and double-pole circuit breakers.

How to Connect Circuit Breakers

1 Shut off the main circuit breaker in the main circuit breaker panel (if you are working in a subpanel, shut off the feeder breaker in the main panel). Remove the panel coverplate, taking care not to touch the parts inside the panel. Test for power (photo, above).

2 Open a knockout in the side of the circuit breaker panel, using a screwdriver and hammer. Attach a cable clamp to the knockout.

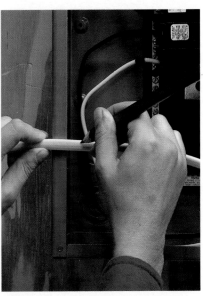

3 Hold cable across the front of the panel near the knockout, and mark sheathing about 1/2" inside the edge of the panel. Strip the cable from marked line to end, using a cable ripper. (There should be 18" to 24" of excess cable.) Insert the cable through the clamp and into the service panel, then tighten the clamp.

4 Bend the bare copper grounding wire around the inside edge of the panel to an open setscrew terminal on the grounding bus bar. Insert the wire into the opening on the bus bar, and tighten the setscrew. Fold excess wire around the inside edge of the panel.

5 For 120-volt circuits, bend the white circuit wire around the outside of the panel to an open setscrew terminal on the neutral bus bar. Clip away excess wire, then strip 1/2" of insulation from the wire, using a combination tool. Insert the wire into the terminal opening, and tighten the setscrew.

6 Strip 1/2" of insulation from the end of the black circuit wire. Insert the wire into the setscrew terminal on a new single-pole circuit breaker, and tighten the setscrew.

7 Slide one end of the circuit breaker onto the guide hook, then press it firmly against the bus bar until it snaps into place. (Breaker installation may vary, depending on the manufacturer.) Fold excess black wire around the inside edge of the panel.

8 **120/240-volt circuits (top):** Connect red and black wires to double-pole breaker. Connect white wire to neutral bus bar, and grounding wire to grounding bus bar. **240-volt circuits (bottom):** Attach white and black wires to double-pole breaker, tagging white wire with black tape. There is no neutral bus bar connection on this circuit.

9 Remove the appropriate breaker knockout on the panel coverplate to make room for the new circuit breaker. A single-pole breaker requires one knockout, while a double-pole breaker requires two knockouts. Reattach the coverplate, and label the new circuit on the panel index.

145

Circuit Maps for 24 Common Wiring Layouts

The arrangement of switches and appliances along an electrical circuit differs for every project. This means that the configuration of wires inside an electrical box can vary greatly, even when fixtures are identical.

The circuit maps on the following pages show the most common wiring variations for typical electrical devices. Most new wiring you install will match one or more of the examples shown. By finding the examples that match your situation, you can use these maps to plan circuit layouts.

The 120-volt circuits shown on the following pages are wired for 15 amps, using 14-gauge wire and receptacles rated at 15 amps. If you are installing a 20-amp circuit, substitute 12-gauge cables and use receptacles rated for 20 amps.

In configurations where a white wire serves as a hot wire instead of a neutral, both ends of the wire are coded with black tape to identify it as hot. In addition, each of the circuit maps shows a box grounding screw. This grounding screw is required in all metal boxes, but plastic electrical boxes do not need to be grounded.

NOTE: For clarity, all grounding conductors in the circuit maps are colored green. In practice, the grounding wires inside sheathed cables usually are bare copper.

Glossary of Electrical Terms

Ampacity: A measurement of how many amps can be safely carried by a wire or cable. Ampacity varies according to the diameter of the wire (page 129).

Common wire: The hot circuit wire that brings current from the power source to a three-way switch, or that carries current from a three-way switch to a light fixture. A common wire is always connected to the darker screw terminal on the switch, sometimes labeled COMMON.

Dedicated circuit: An electrical circuit that serves only one appliance or series of electric heaters.

EMT: *Electrical Metallic Tubing.* A type of metal conduit used for exposed indoor wiring installations, such as wiring in an unfinished basement.

Feeder cable: The length of cable that carries power from the main circuit breaker panel to the first electrical box in a circuit, or from the main panel to a circuit breaker subpanel. Also known as a *home run.*

GFCI: A duplex receptacle or circuit breaker rated as a *Ground-Fault Circuit-Interrupter.* GFCI receptacles provide extra protection against shock and are required by Code in some locations.

Home run: See *Feeder cable*

IMC: *Intermediate Metallic Conduit.* Sturdier than EMT, IMC conduit is used for exposed wiring both indoors and outdoors.

Isolated-ground circuit: A 120-volt circuit installed with three-wire cable that protects sensitive electronic equipment, like a computer, against power surges.

Isolated-ground receptacle: A special-use receptacle, orange in color, with an insulated grounding screw. Used to protect computers or other sensitive electronic equipment against power surges.

Line side wires: Circuit wires that extend "upstream" from an electrical box, toward the power source.

Load side wires: Circuit wires extending "downstream" from an electrical box toward end of circuit.

NM cable: *Non-Metallic sheathed cable.* The standard cable used for indoor wiring inside finished walls.

Pigtail: A short length of wire used to join two or more circuit wires to the same screw terminal on a receptacle, switch, or metal electrical box. Pigtails are color-coded to match the wires they are connected to.

PVC: *Poly-Vinyl Chloride.* A durable plastic used for electrical boxes and conduit. Can be used instead of metal conduit to protect outdoor wiring.

Shared Neutral: When two 120-volt small-appliance circuits are wired using a single three-wire cable, the white circuit wire is a *shared neutral* that serves both circuits.

Split receptacle: A duplex receptacle in which the connecting tab linking the brass screw terminals has been broken. A split receptacle is required when one half of a duplex receptacle is controlled by a switch, or when each half is controlled by a different circuit.

THHN/THWN wires: The type of wire that is recommended for installation inside metal or plastic conduit. Available as individual conductors with color-coded insulation.

Three-wire cable: Sheathed cable with one black, one white, and one red insulated conductor, plus a bare copper grounding wire.

Traveler wires: In a three-way switch configuration, two *traveler wires* run between the pairs of traveler screw terminals on the three-way switches.

Two-wire cable: Sheathed cable with one black and one white insulated conductor plus a bare copper grounding wire.

UF Cable: *Underground Feeder* cable. Used for outdoor wiring, UF cable is rated for direct contact with soil.

1. 120-volt Duplex Receptacles Wired in Sequence

Use this layout to link any number of duplex receptacles in a basic lighting/receptacle circuit. The last receptacle in the cable run is connected like the receptacle shown at the right side of the circuit map below. All other receptacles are wired like the receptacle shown on the left side. Requires two-wire cables.

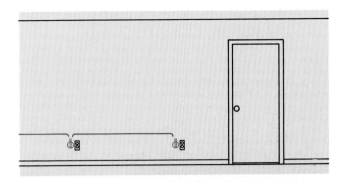

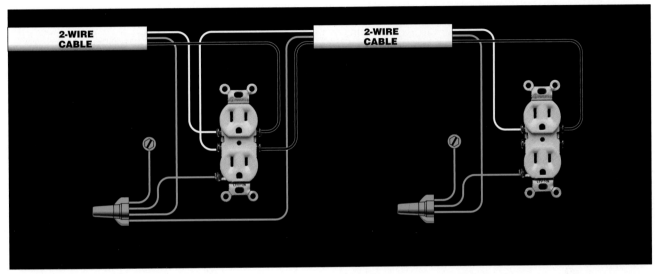

2. GFCI Receptacles (Single-location Protection)

Use this layout when receptacles are within 6 ft. of a water source, like those in kitchens and bathrooms. To prevent "nuisance tripping" caused by normal power surges, GFCIs should be connected only at the LINE screw terminal, so they protect a single location, not the fixtures on the LOAD side of the circuit. Requires two-wire cables. Where a GFCI must protect other fixtures, use circuit map 3.

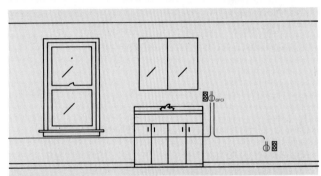

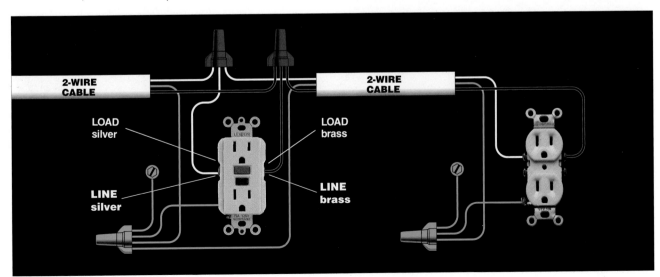

3. GFCI Receptacle, Switch & Light Fixture
(Wired for Multiple-location Protection)

In some locations, such as an outdoor circuit, it is a good idea to connect a GFCI receptacle so it also provides shock protection to the wires and fixtures that continue to the end of the circuit. Wires from the power source are connected to the LINE screw terminals; outgoing wires are connected to LOAD screws. Requires two-wire cables.

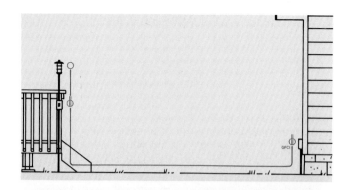

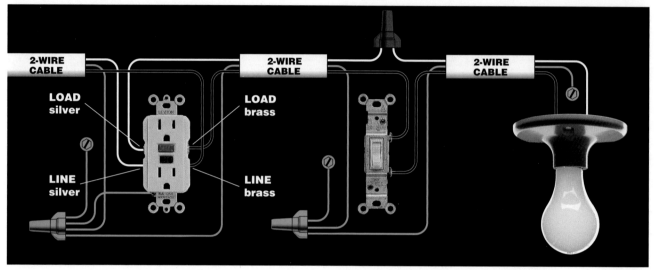

4. Single-pole Switch & Light Fixture
(Light Fixture at End of Cable Run)

Use this layout for light fixtures in basic lighting/receptacle circuits throughout the home. It is often used as an extension to a series of receptacles (circuit map 1). Requires two-wire cables.

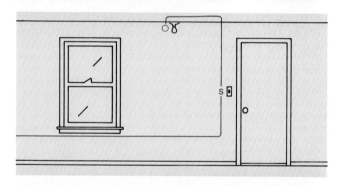

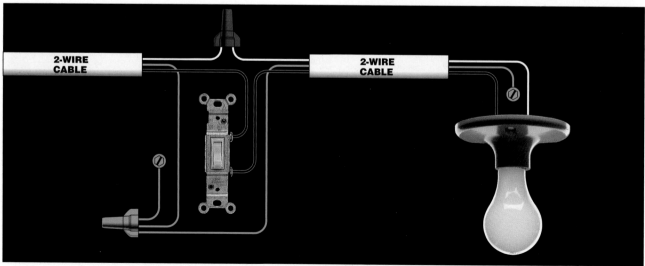

5. Single-pole Switch & Light Fixture (Switch at End of Cable Run)

Use this layout, sometimes called a "switch loop," where it is more practical to locate a switch at the end of the cable run. In the last length of cable, both insulated wires are hot; the white wire is tagged with black tape at both ends to indicate it is hot. Requires two-wire cables.

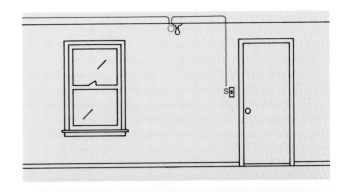

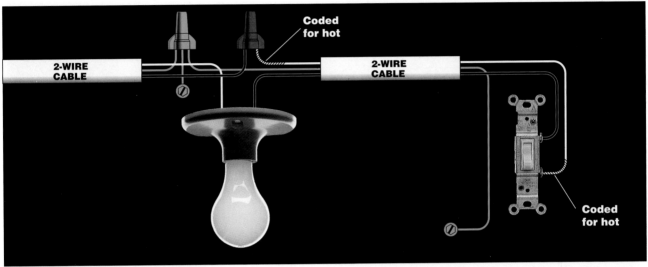

6. Single-pole Switch & Light Fixture, Duplex Receptacle (Switch at Start of Cable Run)

Use this layout to continue a circuit past a switched light fixture to one or more duplex receptacles. To add multiple receptacles to the circuit, see circuit map 1. Requires two-wire and three-wire cables.

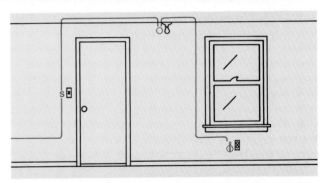

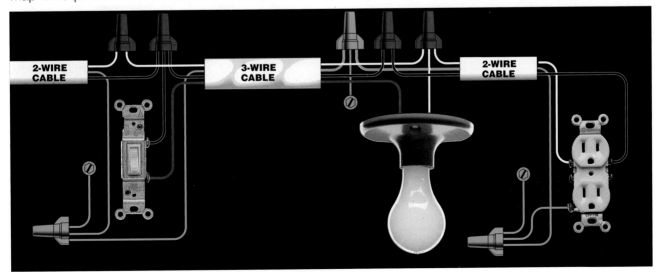

7. Switch-controlled Split Receptacle, Duplex Receptacle (Switch at Start of Cable Run)

This layout lets you use a wall switch to control a lamp plugged into a wall receptacle. This configuration is required by Code for any room that does not have a switch-controlled ceiling fixture. Only the bottom half of the first receptacle is controlled by the wall switch; the top half of the receptacle and all additional receptacles on the circuit are always hot. Requires two-wire and three-wire cables.

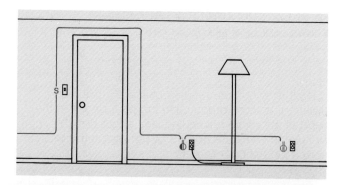

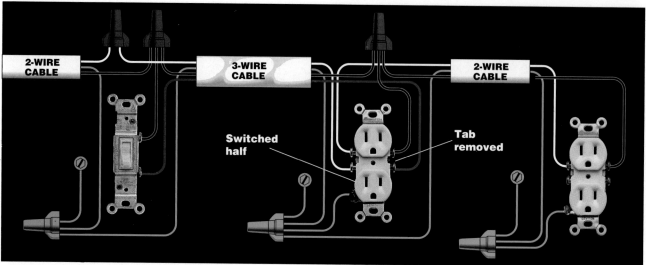

8. Switch-controlled Split Receptacle (Switch at End of Cable Run)

Use this "switch loop" layout to control a split receptacle (see circuit map 7) from an end-of-run circuit location. The bottom half of the receptacle is controlled by the wall switch, while the top half is always hot. White circuit wire attached to the switch is tagged with black tape to indicate it is hot. Requires two-wire cable.

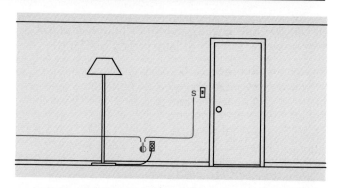

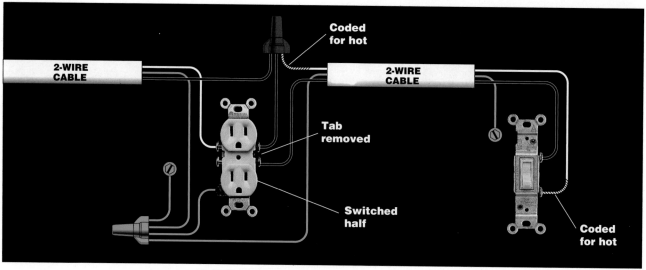

9. Switch-controlled Split Receptacle, Duplex Receptacle (Split Receptacle at Start of Run)

Use this variation of circuit map 7 where it is more practical to locate a switch-controlled receptacle at the start of a cable run. Only the bottom half of the first receptacle is controlled by the wall switch; the top half of the receptacle, and all other receptacles on the circuit, are always hot. Requires two-wire and three-wire cables.

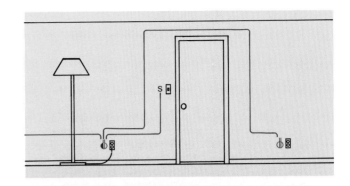

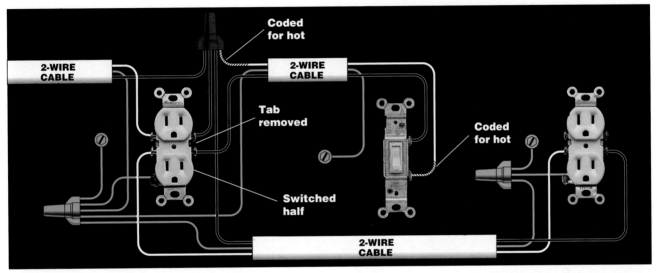

Coded for hot

2-WIRE CABLE

2-WIRE CABLE

Tab removed

Coded for hot

Switched half

2-WIRE CABLE

10. Double Receptacle Circuit with Shared Neutral Wire (Receptacles Alternate Circuits)

This layout features two 120-volt circuits wired with one three-wire cable connected to a double-pole circuit breaker. The black hot wire powers one circuit, the red wire powers the other. The white wire is a shared neutral that serves both circuits. When wired with 12/2 and 12/3 cable, and receptacles rated for 20 amps, this layout can be used for the two small-appliance circuits required in a kitchen.

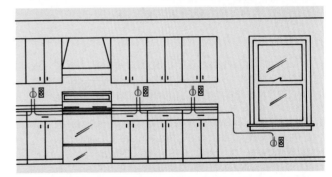

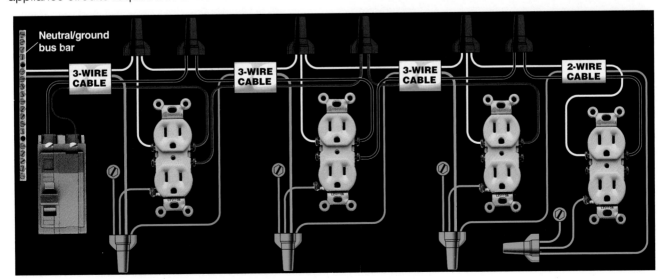

Neutral/ground bus bar

3-WIRE CABLE

3-WIRE CABLE

3-WIRE CABLE

2-WIRE CABLE

11. Double Receptacle Circuit
with GFCIs & Shared Neutral Wire

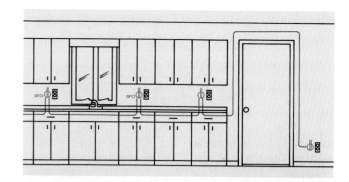

Use this layout variation of circuit map 10 to wire a double receptacle circuit when Code requires that some of the receptacles be GFCIs. The GFCIs should be wired for single-location protection (see circuit map 2). Requires three-wire and two-wire cables.

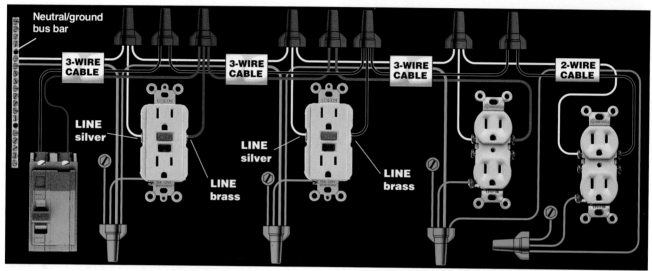

12. 240-volt Appliance Receptacle

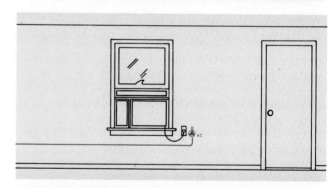

This layout represents a 20-amp, 240-volt dedicated appliance circuit wired with 12/2 cable, as required by Code for a large window air conditioner. Receptacles are available in both singleplex (shown) and duplex styles. The black and white circuit wires connected to a double-pole breaker each bring 120 volts of power to the receptacle. The white wire is tagged with black tape to indicate it is hot.

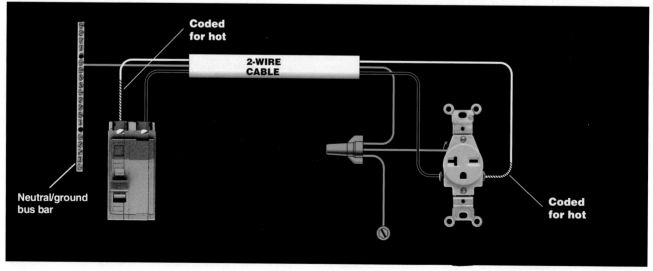

13. 240-volt Baseboard Heaters, Thermostat

This layout is typical for a series of 240-volt baseboard heaters controlled by wall thermostat. Except for the last heater in the circuit, all heaters are wired as shown below. The last heater is connected to only one cable. The size of the circuit and cables are determined by finding the total wattage of all heaters. Requires two-wire cable.

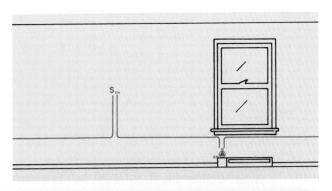

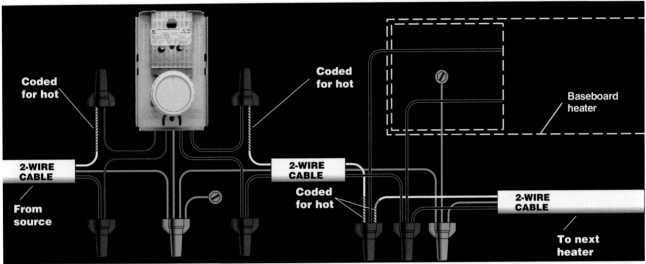

14. 120/240-volt Appliance Receptacle

This layout is for a 50-amp, 120/240-volt dedicated appliance circuit wired with 6/3 cable, as required by Code for a large kitchen range. The black and red circuit wires, connected to a double-pole circuit breaker in the circuit breaker panel, each bring 120 volts of power to the setscrew terminals on the receptacle. The white circuit wire attached to the neutral bus bar in the circuit breaker panel is connected to the neutral setscrew terminal on the receptacle.

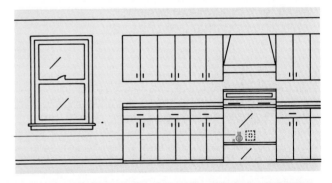

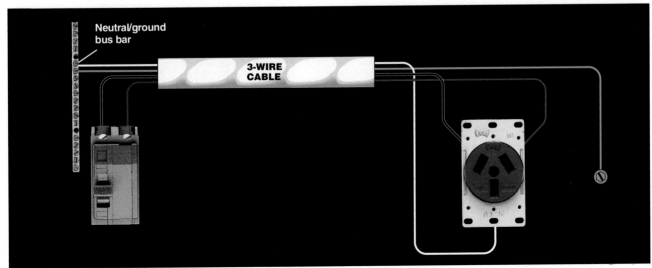

153

15. Dedicated 120-volt Computer Circuit, Isolated-ground Receptacle

This 15-amp circuit provides extra protection against power surges that can harm computers. It uses 14/3 cable in which the red wire serves as an extra grounding conductor. The red wire is tagged with green tape for identification. It is connected to the grounding screw on an "isolated-ground" receptacle, and runs back to the grounding bus bar in the circuit breaker panel without touching any other house wiring.

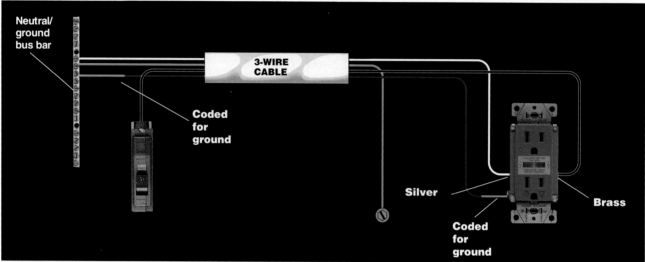

Neutral/ground bus bar

3-WIRE CABLE

Coded for ground

Silver

Brass

Coded for ground

16. Ganged Single-pole Switches Controlling Separate Light Fixtures

This layout lets you place two switches controlled by the same 120-volt circuit in one double-gang electrical box. A single feed cable provides power to both switches. A similar layout with two feed cables can be used to place switches from different circuits in the same box. Requires two-wire cable.

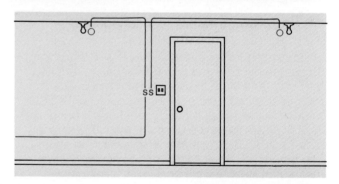

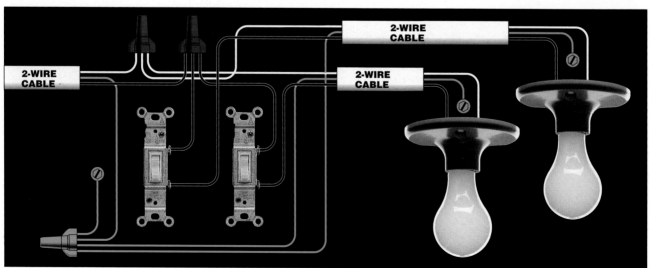

2-WIRE CABLE

2-WIRE CABLE

2-WIRE CABLE

17. Three-way Switches & Light Fixture (Fixture Between Switches)

This layout for three-way switches lets you control a light fixture from two locations. Each switch has one COMMON screw terminal and two TRAVELER screws. Circuit wires attached to the TRAVELER screws run between the two switches, and hot wires attached to the COMMON screws bring current from the power source and carry it to the light fixture. Requires two-wire and three-wire cables.

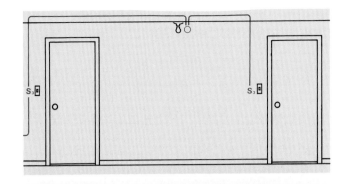

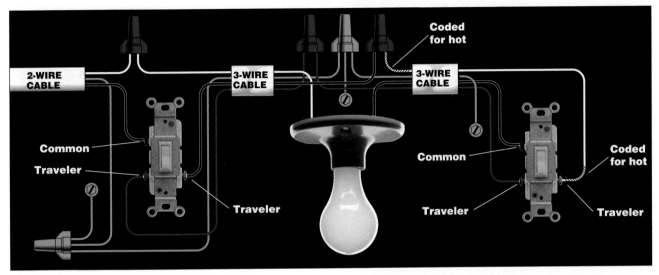

18. Three-way Switches & Light Fixture (Fixture at Start of Cable Run)

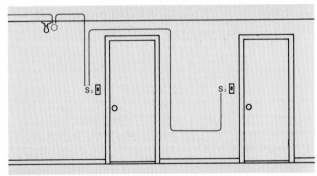

Use this layout variation of circuit map 17 where it is more convenient to locate the fixture ahead of the three-way switches in the cable run. Requires two-wire and three-wire cables.

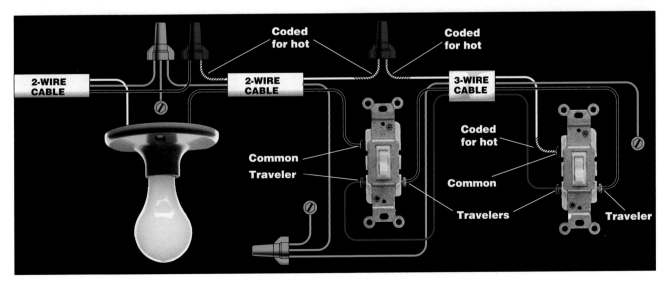

19. Three-way Switches & Light Fixture (Fixture at End of Cable Run)

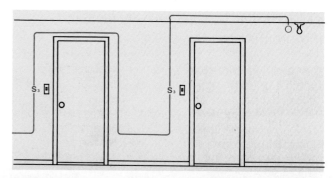

This alternate variation of the three-way switch layout (circuit map 17) is used where it is more practical to locate the fixture at the end of the cable run. Requires two-wire and three-wire cables.

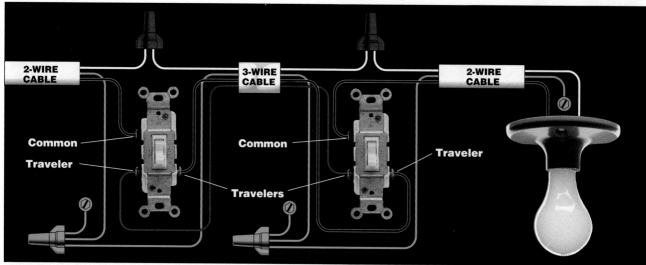

20. Three-way Switches & Light Fixture with Duplex Receptacle

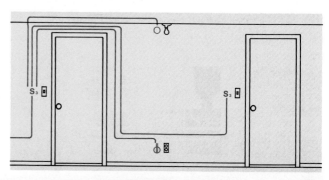

Use this layout to add a receptacle to a three-way switch configuration (circuit map 17). Requires two-wire and three-wire cables.

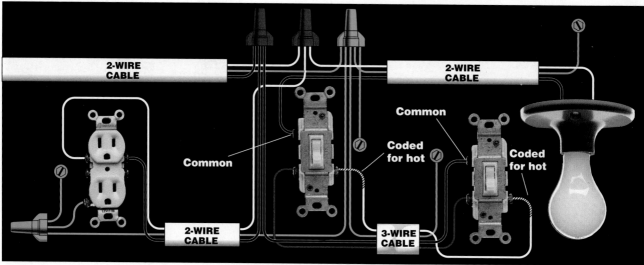

21. Ceiling Fan/Light Fixture Controlled by Ganged Switches (Fan at End of Cable Run)

This layout is for a combination ceiling fan/light fixture, controlled by a speed-control switch and dimmer in a double-gang switch box. Requires two-wire and three-wire cables.

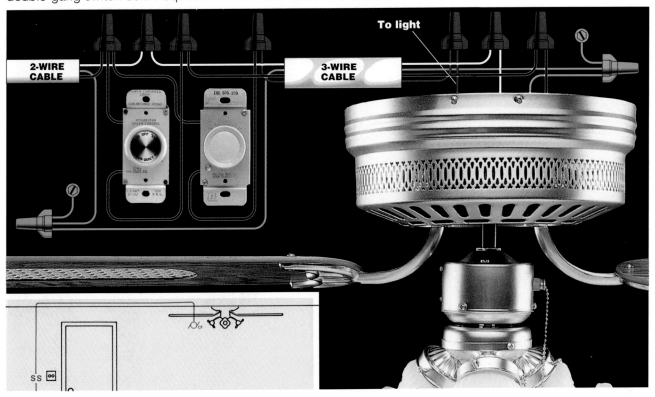

22. Ceiling Fan/Light Fixture Controlled by Ganged Switches (Switches at End of Cable Run)

Use this "switch loop" layout variation when it is more practical to install the ganged speed control and dimmer switches for the ceiling fan at the end of the cable run. Requires two-wire and three-wire cables.

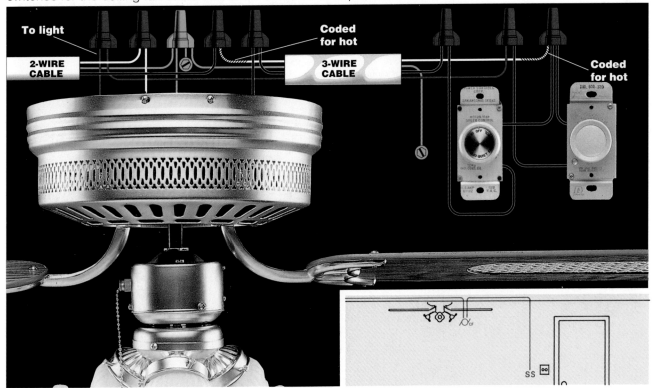

Index

A

ABS pipes and fittings, 86-88, 102-103, 114, 116
  see also: Plastic pipes and fittings
Adhesives, 72-77
  chart of various types, 72
  homemade glue applicators, 73
  hot glue, 76-77
  removing adhesives, 74-75
  solvent-based vs. water-based, 73
Air-conditioning, circuit map, 152
Air-powered nailer, 46
Aluminum wire, 130
Ampacity, 128
  circuit breaker amperage, 144
  main service rating, 143
  wire gauge/wattage load, 129
  see also: specific appliances
Asbestos, safety precautions, 75
Augers (snakes), 84-85

B

Backer board, 26
Ball peen hammer, 83
Band clamps, homemade, 60, 67
  see also: Rope clamps
Banded coupling, 89, 114, 116-117
Band saw, mounting to portable workbench, 70
Bar clamps, storing and using, 64
Baseboard heater,
  circuit map, 153
  installing circuit, 124, 135
Basement wiring, 146
  conduit for wiring, 138-139
  electrical boxes for, 122, 140
Bathroom wiring,
  GFCI receptacles required, 125, 147
  switch locations, 127
Beeswax, 15
Belt sanders, 22, 78
  see also: Power tools, Sanding
Bench grinder,
  mounting to portable workbench, 70
  sharpening tool blades, 20-21
Bench vise, 61, 63, 64
Bending flexible copper pipe, 91
Bit extension, 25
Black iron, 110
Black oxide screwdriver tip, 13
Blades, see: Chisels, Planes, Saw blades
Boards,
  center marker for, 55
  cutting, 17, 38, 40
  dividing into equal parts, 51
  drawing line parallel to edge, 54
  marking for rough cut, 49
  ripping, 29, 33-34
Box,
  checking for square, 53
  electrical, cutting around, 57
  see also: Electrical boxes
Brad pusher, 12
Branch circuits, 142-143
Brass plumbing parts, 86-87
  compression fittings, 98
  flare fittings, 100
  soldering brass valves, 96
Bus bars in circuit breaker panel, 142-143

C

Cabinets,
  building four-corner miter clamp, 68-69
  checking for square, 53
Cable, 128-129
  see also: Coaxial cable, NM cable, UF cable
Cable ripper, 120, 132-134, 144
Cable television jack, 128
Cast-iron pipes, 86-87
  connecting to other materials, 89, 114, 116-117
  cutting, 85, 87, 114, 116

removing and replacing, 115-117
  working with cast iron, 114-117
Cat's paw, 8
Caulk guns, 9, 82
Caulking with hot glue gun, 77
C-clamps, 8
  clamping frames, 62
  clamping molding in miter saw, 65
  clamping repaired wood, 73-74
  clamping stop blocks on miter saw, 41
  clamping tools to bench, 38
  extending reach, 60
  padding jaws, 62
  using with angle irons, 63
  using with fingerboards, 36
  using with rope clamps, 67
  using with routers, 44
Ceiling fan/light fixture,
  circuit maps, 157
  electrical boxes for, 122-123, 126
Centering,
  finding center of circular piece, 50
  finding center of workpiece, 55
Center punch, 7
Chair legs, clamping, 60
Chalk line, 8, 47
Chisels, 7-8, 18-19
  sharpening, 20-21
  storage tips, 6
  using to remove dried adhesive, 75
Chromed brass plumbing parts, 86-87
Chromed copper pipes, 86-87
Chuck (power drill), 24
Circles,
  cutting with router, 44
  drawing, 49, 51
  finding center of circular piece, 50
Circuit breaker panel, 142-143
  panel index, 145
  safety precautions, 132, 141-144
  testing for power, 120, 144
Circuit breakers,
  feeder breaker, 142
  installing, 144-145
  main circuit breaker, 142, 144
  slimline breakers, 142
Circuit breaker subpanel, 142-144
Circuit maps, 146-157
Circuit overload, 142
Circuits,
  branch circuits, 142-143
  code requirements, 119
  120/240-volt circuit breaker connection, 142-143, 146-157
  120-volt circuit breaker connection, 142-143
  240-volt circuit breaker connection, 143
Circuit test, 82
Circuit tester, see: Neon circuit tester
Circular saws, 9, 28-31
  building a straightedge guide for, 30
  building a triangle guide for, 31
  see also: Power saws, Power tools
Clamping, 60-71
  building four-corner miter clamp, 68-69
  clamping delicate workpieces, 64
  padding clamp jaws, 61-62
  using inner tubes as clamps, 60-61, 67
  using jumper-cable jaws as clamps, 61
  using pliers as clamps, 61-62
Clamps,
  tips for using, 58-59
  see: specific clamp types
Closet auger, 84
Coaxial cable, 128
Coil-spring tubing bender, 91
Cold chisel, 82
Combination square, 8, 54
Combination tool, 120
Common screw on three-way switch, 155-156
Common wire, definition, 146
Compass, homemade, 49, 51
Compression fittings, 90-91, 98-99, 103
Computer receptacle wiring, 119, 146
  circuit map, 154
Concrete, anchors, 15

Concrete, attaching framing to, 46
Conduit, 138-141
  installing on masonry walls, 140-141
  see also: Flexible metal conduit, Rigid metal conduit
Connecting pipes, 88-89
Connecting wires,
  pigtailing, 131
  push-in fittings, 130
  screw terminals, 130
  wire nuts, 131
Coping saw, 9
Copper pipes and fittings, 86-90
  bending pipes, 91
  connecting to other materials, 89, 102, 104
  cutting pipes, 92-93
  flexible copper pipe, 86-87, 90-91, 93, 98-101
  grades of copper, 90-91
  rigid copper pipe, 86-87, 90-91, 93
  soldering, 90, 92, 94-97
Cordless power screwdriver, 13
Corner clamp, 58
Corroded pipes and fittings, 110-113
  removing and replacing, 111-113
Counterbore pilot hole, 13
Coupling nut, 89
Couplings, 88
CPVC pipes and fittings, 86-88, 102-103
  see also: Plastic pipes and fittings
Crosscuts, building triangle guide, 31
Crosscut saw, 8
Cutting oil, 25

D

Dadoes,
  cutting with circular saw, 29
  cutting with router and T-square, 45
Decorative edgings, router techniques, 42-43
Dedicated circuit, definition, 146
Depth stop for drills, 25
Diagramming circuits, circuit maps, 146-157
Diameter of workpiece, finding, 55
Dielectric union, 89
Dimmer switch, 157
Disc sander, 23
Doors, clamping, 64-66, 71
Double-gang electrical box, 154, 157
Double-pole circuit breaker,
  connection variation for 120/240-volt circuit, 145
  installing, 144-145
  kitchen range, 153
Double receptacle circuit, circuit map, 151-152
Dowels, 61, 75, 78
Drain system, materials, 86-87, 90, 102-103, 114
Drain-waste-vent system, 87-88, 103
  fittings, 88
Drawers, checking for square, 53
Drill bits, 8, 25-27
  bit extension, 25
  sharpening, 27
Drilling tips, 25-26
Drills, 7, 14, 24-27, 85
  guide accessories, 25
  hammer drill, 46
  hand drills, 24
  power drills, 24
  using as disc sander, 79
  using as flap sander, 78
  see also: Drill bits, Power tools
Duplex receptacles, see: Receptacles
DWV system, see: Drain-waste-vent system

E

Eggbeater drills, 24
Elbow fittings, 88
Electrical boxes, 122-123
  cutting around, 57
  for conduit wiring, 138-139
  installing, 124-127
Electrical cable, see: Cable
Electrical loads, evaluating, 143
Electrical metallic tubing, see: EMT
Electrical system, grounding to plumbing, 102
Electric heater, see: Baseboard heater, Blower-heater

Electronic level, 52
Electronic stud finder, 8
EMT (electrical metallic tubing), 139, 146

F
Fasteners, 12-15
Feeder cable, 143, 146
Files, 7, 83
Fingerboards for table saw, making, 36-37
Finished walls, running cable inside, 128
Finish nail, 15
Fish tape, 121, 136-137, 141
Fittings,
  compression, 90-91, 98-99, 103
  drain-waste-vent, 88
  flare, 90-91, 100-101
  grip, 89, 103-104, 108-109
  hubbed cast iron, 114
  soldered, 90, 92, 94-97
  solvent-glued plastic, 103-104, 106-108
  transition, 88-89, 102
  water supply, 88
Flap sander, 23, 78
Flare fittings, 90-91, 100-101
Flaring tool, 91
  connecting flexible copper pipe, 100-101
Flexible copper pipe, 86-87, 90, 98-101
  bending, 91
  cutting, 93
Flexible metal conduit, 138
  electrical boxes for, 122
  see also: Conduit
Flexible plastic pipe, 102-104
  cutting, 104, 108
  fitting, 108-109
Fluorescent light fixture, installing, 124, 135
Four-corner miter clamp, building, 68-69
Four-pair telephone cable, 128
Frame,
  checking for square, 53
  clamping, 62, 68-69
Framing square, 8

G
Galvanized iron pipes and fittings, 86-88, 110-113
  connecting to other materials, 89, 102
  removing and replacing, 111-113
Galvanized metal, cutting, 38
Ganged switches, 154
Gas lines, 90, 100
GFCI (ground-fault circuit-interrupter), 146
  circuit maps, 147-148
Glue, see: Adhesives
Glue guns, 7, 9
Gluing, see: Adhesives, Clamping
Grinder, see: Bench grinder
Grip fittings, 89, 103-104, 108-109
Grip-it® twist anchors, 13
Grounding bus bar, 142-143
Grounding clip, 135, 138
Grounding conductor in circuit breaker panel, 142
Grounding electrical system to plumbing, 102
Grounding screw, 131, 135, 146
Grounding wire,
  for circuit breaker panel, 142
  identifying, 146, 154
  in cable, 128
  installing in conduit, 138-139

H
Hacksaw, 82
Hammer drill, 46
Hammers, 7-8
Hand auger, 84
Hand drills, 24
Hand sanding block, 22
Handsaws, 16-17
Handscrew clamps,
  using to anchor tools to workbench, 64
  using to make rope clamp, 65
Handscrews, 58
Hand tools,
  storage tips, 6, 16
  see also: specific types of hand tools
Hardwood, predrilling, 12

Heat gun, 85
Hex-head sheetmetal screw, 13
Hi-low screw, 13
Hot glue gun, 7, 9, 76-77
Hot water transition fitting, 89
Hot wire, definition, 146
Humidity levels, controlling, 6

I
Icemaker on refrigerator, 89
IMC (intermediate metallic conduit), 139, 146
  installing, 139
Intermediate metallic conduit, see: IMC
Iron pipes,
  cutting, 38
  see also: Black iron, Cast-iron pipes, Galvanized
    iron pipes and fittings, Pipes
Isolated-ground receptacle, 146
  circuit map, 154

J
Jigs,
  for finding center of workpiece, 50, 55
  for leveling warped lumber, 53
Jig saw, 9
  using to cut around electrical box, 57
  see also: Power saws, Power tools

K
Kitchen wiring, switch recommendations, 127

L
Lag screw, 13
Laminate trimmer, 43
Large-appliance cable, 128
Layout, see: Marking, Measuring
Layout tools, 47
Lead anchors, 15
Levels, 7-8, 52-53
Light fixtures,
  circuit maps, 148-149, 154-156
  electrical boxes for, 122-124, 126
  installing between joists, 126
Line side wire, definition, 146
Load, see: Electrical loads
Load side wire, definition, 146

M
Magnetic screwdriver, 13
Main waste and vent stack, 86-87
Mallet, 8
Marking, 49-57
  drawing circles, 49, 51
  drawing line parallel to edge of board, 54
  marking boards for rough cuts, 49
  marking protrusions, 57
  see also: Measuring, Patterns for projects
Masking tape, protecting drill hole, 26
Masonry, anchors, 15
Measuring, 49-57
  dividing boards into equal parts, 51
  finding center of circular piece, 50
  measuring inside drawer or box, 50
Measuring tools, 47
Metal, cutting, 38
Metal conduit, see: Conduit
Miter box, power, 46, 85, 105
Miter clamp, 68-69
Miters,
  building four-corner miter clamp, 68-69
  clamping molding in miter saw, 65
  mitering crown and cove molding, 39
Miter saw, see: Power miter saw
Miter stop block, 41
Molding, mitering, 39
Mortise, chisel techniques, 18-19

N
Nailing, 10-11
Nail puller, making nail notch in claw hammer, 10
Nails, 12
National Electrical Code, 119
Neon circuit tester, 120, 144
NM (nonmetallic) sheathed cable, 128-129, 146

installing, 132-137
  installing inside finished walls, 136-137
  see also: Feeder cable, UF cable
Nonmetallic sheathed cable, see: NM cable

O
Oakum, 114
Offset screwdriver, 13
120/240-volt circuit breaker connection, 143
120-volt circuit breaker connection, 142-143
Outdoor wiring, circuit map, 148

P
Palm sander, 9
Paneling,
  cutting tips, 30, 57
  handling tips, 65
Pan-head sheetmetal screw, 13
Patterns for projects, 54-57
  making rubbing of object, 55
  making story pole, 54
  marking identical measurements on multiple
    pieces, 54
  marking on metal or glass, 57
  transferring to workpiece, 54, 56
  using contact paper, 57
  using photocopy to transfer pattern, 56
  see also: Marking, Measuring
PB pipes, 86-87, 102-103
  see also: Plastic pipes and fittings
Permits for wiring projects, 119
Phillips screwdriver, 8, 13
Pigtail,
  connecting wires with, 131
  definition, 146
Pilot holes, 14
  drilling with finish nail, 42
  for screws, 15
Pipe clamps, 59, 64-67
  storing, 65
Pipes,
  clamping in bench vise, 61, 63
  clamping in portable workbench, 70
  cutting, 38, 40
  see also: Cast-iron pipes, Copper pipes and
    fittings, Galvanized iron pipes and fittings,
    Plastic pipes and fittings
Pipe wrench, 85
Planes, 9, 18-21
  sharpening, 20-21
Planning wiring projects, 146-157
  code requirements, 119
Plastic concrete anchors, 15
Plastic pipes and fittings, 86-88, 102-103
  connecting to other materials, 89, 102, 104, 114,
    116 117
  cutting pipes, 40, 104-105, 108
  flexible plastic pipe, 86-87, 102-104, 108-109
  gluing, 104, 106-108
  ratings, 103
  rigid plastic pipe, 86-87, 102-109
  see also: ABS pipes and fittings, CPVC pipes
    and fittings, PB pipes, PVC pipes and fittings
Plastic tubing cutter, 84
Pliers, 61-62, 83
Plumb bob/chalk line, 8
Plumbing materials, 86-87
Plumbing tools, 82-85
Plywood, clamping sheets of plywood, 65
Portable workbench, 70-71
Power drills, 8, 24
  drilling tips, 25-26
  see also: Drills
Power miter saw, 38-41
  blade types, 38
  checking blade alignment, 34, 39
  clamping molding in place, 65
  making flip-out stop block, 41
  see also: Power saws, Power tools
Power sander, see: Belt sander, Disc sander,
  Palm sander, Sanding
Power saws,
  blade types, 38
  see also: Power tools, specific types of power saws

Power tools,
    clamping to workbench, 38, 64
    see also: specific types of power tools
Propane torch, 85, 95
Pushstick for table saw, making, 35
Putty knives, 8, 83
PVC (poly-vinyl chloride), 146
    conduit, 139
    electrical boxes, 122
PVC pipes and fittings, 86-88, 102-103, 114, 116
    see also: Plastic pipes and fittings

R
Rabbet grooves, cutting with circular saw, 29
Range circuit,
    circuit map, 153
Ratchet screwdriver, 13
Receptacles,
    120-volt, circuit maps, 147-154, 157
    120-volt, code requirements, 119
    120-volt, in basements, 140
    120-volt, installing boxes for, 125, 140
    120-volt, *see also:* GFCI, Isolated-ground
        receptacle, Split receptacle, Switched receptacle
Reciprocating saws, 46, 85, 87, 110-111
Reducers, 88
Right-angle drill, 85
Rigid metal conduit, 139
    see also: Conduit, Outdoor wiring
Ripping boards,
    with circular saw, 29
    with table saw, 33-34
Riser clamp, 115
Room size, measuring, 53
Rope clamps, making, 65, 67
Round-head wood screw, 13
Router bits, 42-43
Routers, 9, 44-45
    see also: Power tools
Router table,
    mounting to portable workbench, 70
Rust, preventing on tools, 6, 38

S
Saddle valve, 89
Safety,
    preventing circuit overloads, 142
    preventing shock, 146, 148
    storing equipment, 77
    when working in main panel, 132, 141-144
Sanding, 78-80
    clamping power sander to workbench, 64
    making disc sander, 79
    making flap sander, 78
    see also: Power sander
Sanding belt, cleaning, 78
Sanding block, 8, 22
Sanding drums, 23
Sanding tools, 22-23
Sandpaper, 23, 78-80
    see also: Sanding
Sanitary T, fitting, 88
Saw blades, 38
    alignment of blade, 33-34
    sharpness, 16
Sawhorses, 60
Saws,
    circular, 9
    coping saw, 9
    crosscut, 8
    jig saw, 9
    reciprocating, 46
    table, 46
    wallboard, 8
Screwdrivers, 13-14, 83, 85
    cordless, 8, 13
Screw holder, 13
Screws, 13-14
    tips for driving, 13, 15
Service wires in main service panel, 142-143
Shared neutral in small-appliance circuits, 146, 151-152
Sharpening,
    chisels and hand planes, 20-21
    drill bits, 27

handsaws, 16
Shock protection, 146, 148
Shutoff valves, 89
    attaching to supply tubes, 98-99
Single-pole circuit breaker, 143-145
    circuit maps, 148-149, 154
Slimline circuit breaker, 142
Slot screwdriver, 13
Snake (auger), 84-85
Snap cutter, 114, 116
Soldering,
    brass valves, 96
    copper pipes and fittings, 90, 92, 94-96
    taking apart soldered joints, 97
Solvent-glued fittings, 103
Solvent-gluing plastic pipe, 104, 106-108
Sonic measuring tools, 53, 120
Spindles,
    clamping, 66
    sanding, 79
Spiral ratchet drill, 24
Split receptacle,
    circuit maps, 150-151
    defined, 146
Spring clamps,
    using jumper cables as, 61
    using pliers as, 61
Spud wrench, 84
Square, *see:* Combination square
Squaring, checking projects for square, 53
Stairway, installing light fixture, 126
Steel, cutting, 38
Steel beam, fastening wood to, 15
Story pole for transferring measurements, 54
Straddle stick for table saw, making, 35
Straightedge guide for circular saw, 30
Strap clamp, 59
Strip gauge, 130
Stripping cable and wire, 130
Stubby screwdriver, 13
Stud driver, 46
Subpanel, 142-144
Supply tubes, *see:* Water supply lines
Sweating, *see:* Soldering
Switch-controlled light fixture,
    circuit maps, 148-151, 154-156
    code requirements, 119
Switches, 119
    circuit maps, 148-151, 154-157
    electrical boxes for, 127
Switch loop, 149-150, 157

T
Table saws, 32-37, 46
    checking blade alignment, 33-34
    making fingerboard, 36-37
    making pushstick, 35
    making straddle stick, 35
    setting blade height, 33
    see also: Power saws, Power tools
Tack hammer, 12
Tape measure, 8, 49-50
    waxing metal blade, 6
T-bevel, 8, 47
Telephone outlet wiring, cable, 128
Television jack, *see:* Cable television jack
Testing for power,
    neon circuit tester, 120
    when working in circuit breaker panel, 142-144
T-fittings, 88
Thermostat for electric heaters,
    circuit map, 153
    electrical box for, 127
THHN/THWN wire, 128, 146
Threaded adapter, 89
Three-way clamp, 58
Three-way switches, 146
    circuit maps, 155-156
Three-wire cable, 128, 146, 149-157
Tiled walls, and installation of electrical boxes, 127
Timbers, cutting with circular saw, 28
Toenailing, 12
Tool boxes, 9
Tools, 6-12, 17, 20-21, 27-47
    basic collection, 8-9

for electrical wiring, 120-121
for plumbing, 82-85
for special jobs, 46
intermediate collection, 9
layout, measuring, 47
power specifications, 9
    see also: Hand tools, Power tools, specific tools
Tourniquet clamp, making, 62
Transition fittings, 88-89, 102
Traps, 103
Traveler screw on three-way switches, circuit maps, 155-156
Traveler wire, definition, 146
Triangle guide for circular saw, 31
Triple-gang electrical boxes, 122
Tubing bender, 91
Tubing cutter, 84, 87, 92-93, 105
Two-wire cable, 146, 128
    circuit maps, 147-157

U
UF (underground feeder) cable, 128, 146
Under-cabinet lights, 124
Underground feeder cable, *see:* UF cable
Upgrading electrical service, 143
Utility knife, 8
Utility wallboard screws, 13

V
Valves, 86-87
    soldering brass valves, 96
    see also: Shutoff valves
Veneer, regluing, 74
Vent fan, 124
Vent pipes, 86-87, 114
    see also: Drain-waste-vent system, Main waste and vent stack
Vise, *see:* Bench vise
Vise-Grip®, 59

W
Wall anchors, 15
Wallboard saw, 8
Wallboard screwgun, 13
Wallboard screws, 13
Wall studs, checking warped lumber for level, 53
Waste stack, *see:* Main waste and vent stack
Waste-T, fitting, 88, 105
Water pressure problems, 110
Water supply lines, 86-87, 102-103
    attaching to shutoff valves, 89, 98-99
    copper, 90
    galvanized iron, 110
Water supply system, fittings, 88
Wattage, maximum wattage of wire gauges, 129
Weatherproof electrical boxes, 122-123
Window screen, uses for, 80
Wire connections,
    pigtailing two or more wires, 131
    push-in fittings, 130
    screw terminals, 130
    wire nuts, 131
Wire nuts, 129, 131
Wires, 128-129
    connecting, 130-131
    stripping, 130
    see also: Service wires
Wiring diagram, *see:* Diagramming circuits
Wonderbar®, 8
Wood,
    buttons, 14
    drilling tips, 25-26
    tips for driving screws, 13, 15
Wood clamps, *see:* Clamping, specific types of clamps
Wood splinters, repairing, 73
Workbench,
    clamping tools to bench, 38, 64, 70
    portable, 70-71
    replacing bench top, 71
Workmate® portable gripping bench, 59
Workshop,
    controlling humidity levels, 6
    techniques, 49-57, 60-80
Wrenches, types, 82-85